YOU HAVE NOT A LEG TO STAND ON

D.D. MAYERS

Published in 2015 by
Andrews UK Limited
www.andrewsuk.com

Contents

Disaster	1
Hello Babe	8
Bangalore	12
Such Unkindness - Blessed Oceans	18
Stoke Mandeville	22
New York and Colorado	29
Africa	35
Rotherhithe	40
Storm and Stuttgart	45
Prep School	53
Kidnapped	62
English Channel	70
The Tutor	75
London	79
Nairobi	83
Mombasa to Jericho	91
Damascus to Hamburg	104
Back to London	122
Passion for Kenya	133
The Vineyard	142
Breaking down	149
Uncle Peter	156
Home Alone	163

I dedicate this book to my wife. You will quickly realise, for the last 39 years, she has both literally and metaphorically, carried me around the world and through my life. Since the moment she found me in a little African hospital in central Kenya at midnight on the 29th of June 1976, she has been my other self. She is my heart and soul and means more to me than I can possibly express.

I would also like to thank, from the bottom of my heart, both our families and all friends for their unerring acceptance of my plight and never once shying away from any support we have needed.

YOU HAVE NOT A LEG
TO STAND ON

Disaster

The day started off just like any other day, a beautiful day. Every day in the Kedong Valley was a beautiful day. The Kedong Valley nestles in the side of the Great Rift Valley that carves its way through the East of Africa, starting in South Africa and ends engulfing The Red Sea. I was 32, my wife 18 months younger. We'd been married for eight years. It's a long time ago, as I write this, but I'm told we were an attractive couple. We lived here in this beautiful place where the Kedong River bubbles up out of the ground; millions of gallons a day of crystal clear water. When people see the garden for the first time, their breath is taken away, and they'd whisper 'Shangri-La.' But by the end of this beautiful day, the 29th of June 1976, our lives will have turned upside down, and it would be the start of years and years of desperate, traumatic despair.

The butcher arrived on time, and he said 'Let's go in my car so we can talk.' It was a spanking new Volvo, much nicer than my poor old Peugeot. 'Great.' I jumped in. He'd seen the herd before but he wanted to see them once more before paying in cash. He intended to obtain the licence to walk them from their grazing in the north of the country to his slaughterhouse in Nairobi.

It was a pleasant drive. We chatted about how he'd become so successful. Even then, seventeen years after independence, it was unusual for an African, if he weren't a politician, to be a successful businessman.

We arrived just before five in the hot, dusty, ramshackle little wooden township of Rumeruti, where the police station was the only stone building. 'Hello, hello, how are you all, is the licence ready?' 'Yes, yes, sign here.' 'Thanks very much.' I jumped back in. It was now about three minutes before the crash would happen.

The road was quite good; it was a murram road, a dirt road, with loose gravel in the middle and on the sides. You could drive quite fast when keeping to the tracks but needed skill if you came out of them. We were moving quite quickly, a bit too quickly. We were coming up to a sharp bend to the right. The wheels caught the gravel in the middle and the side on the left. The car started to drift. He'd lost control, I instinctively reached for the dashboard, mistake, a split-second later... oblivion.

***

With the impact of the accident, that moment of oblivion, I could easily have died. People breezily say 'you're lucky to be alive.' I usually just say 'Yes' but I think, 'what the hell do you know, you stupid ill-informed idiot.'

They say this to me while looking at me sitting in my wheelchair, knowing I've been bound to this contraption since 1976 and will be for the rest of my life. Not only can I never walk again but I'm doubly incontinent, impotent and in continuous, excruciating pain below the level of the break, meaning normal painkilling drugs have no effect. I know this must seem as though I'm 'bitter and twisted', but I'm very aware of how much others can put up with, so I never give that impression. My wife is the only person who has any perception of how I think and feel about being alive.

I've reread this last paragraph I wrote some months ago, and I think I should, at this point, expand upon the devastating effect paraplegia has on an individual.

Not being able to walk could be described as really the least of the problems. If it were that alone, then coming to terms with using some sort of contraption to move about, would quickly be overcome. The choice of wheelchairs to cars, and financial assistance from social services is overwhelming. Even impotence doesn't necessarily mean you can't have a fulfilling, close relationship with the opposite sex, or the same sex for that matter.

It's incontinence that buggers you up. Incontinence and the consequences of incontinence are unacceptable both socially and individually. It's only in the last few years that 'urinary tract infection' is openly discussed. And yet before the advent of antibiotics, as recently as after the end of the Second World War, the average life expectancy for a paraplegic was about three years.

So now you'll live and not die. But what's the point of living if, as a human being and not an animal, you have no control over your bowels and bladder. It's that most basic of functions that differentiate us from all other animals.

When I left Stoke Mandeville hospital, my shopping list for the management of urine collection was unusual. It included one kipper (a thick rubber urine bag that looked like a kipper, which you tied to your leg) and a yard of half-inch yellow rubber tubing. There was also a spigot, a tube of white rubber glue, a needle and a bag of condoms. However carefully I assembled this extraordinary collection of disparate items required to stick the condom to my deflated, flaccid, useless penis, there seemed to be a major 'accident'. Hatefully this occurred on average, about once a week. For the record, I'll describe to you what an 'accident' actually entails.

***

We were invited to stay for a few days with a lifetime friend of my wife's family, at his beautiful castle in Scotland. He was blind and had been so for most of his adult life. Nevertheless the castle was immaculate, both inside and out, and he ran the vast estate with the most up-to-date methods available for the day.

The Laird was waiting for us at the top of the long grey stone staircase. He was a big man, not fat, big, quite tall, bald top of his head with white hair above his ears. He wore the Stuart tartan kilt he always wore when in Scotland, and the traditional green tweed short jacket, and knee-length woollen stockings with thick leather brogues.

The staff were assembled to carry me up the baronial staircase and into the main hall. It was magnificent. Just what you'd expect a hall of a beautiful castle would look like. He'd recently rewired, cleaned and painted the entire inside of the castle. We were led to our room by the Laird himself, turning the lights on and off as we processed from room to room. He gave us detailed descriptions of all he'd had done and how it looked before the work started. Listening to him, you would never have known he'd been completely blind for more than thirty years. We finally reached our room which he'd also recently updated. It was stunning; an enormous four-poster bed facing a roaring log fire and a magnificent view over lovely parkland. This was dotted with long-horned, shaggy Highland cattle, lying or standing around among imposing, sweeping, tall beech and oak trees. A scene you would have thought had long gone, or only as a showcase, not to live in for every day. After tea in the 'long drawing-room', with fires at both ends, my wife took me along to the rooms she used to stay in, as a child and teenager, every Easter holiday. The main impression I got, although I'd never been in a castle before, was how homely it felt. For giants, but definitely cozy! My wife and the Laird obviously had much to catch up on. They hadn't spoken since before we were married. He'd given her a wedding present of a diamond tiara which also became a stunning necklace. All her nieces have worn it for their weddings. The time flew.

A staff member came in and suggested we might like to go to our room to change before dinner, not knowing the enormous energy and teamwork required.

The Laird's favourite tipple was a large whisky in a long glass, topped up to the brim, with Guinness. I don't know why I hadn't thought of it before! We didn't have wine with our food, we went on with the same thing. I can't really remember what we had to eat. I suppose it must have been a haunch of venison off the estate. It was a good thing I was sitting in a wheelchair otherwise I think I'd have disgraced myself and fallen flat on my face.

After much reminiscing and affectionate laughter, of which I, thankfully, was not a part, we finally wound our weary way back to our lovely warm room, me with a full bladder.

In those days, to empty my bladder, I'd have to tap it with my fingers for a minute or so. Then my wife, with clenched fists and arms locked straight, would lean on it, with all the weight she could muster. The urine would then spurt out, into the condom, down the rubber pipe and into the collection bag on my leg. At night, I'd disconnect the tube from the leg bag and connect it to a bigger bag which I'd hang on the side of the bed. All very romantic you understand. But tonight there was nothing to hang the bag on, so I had to leave it on the floor. The bed was a castle sized bed, for giants, so I was a long way off the ground. Clambering, or perhaps climbing, into a giant's bed, wasn't on the agenda at Stoke Mandeville. Anyway, I got there in the end and went out like a light. 'The accident' I've been leading up to is only a couple of hours away from happening. I awoke with a start. I instinctively felt the sheets, they were soaking wet. 'Oh no,' I half shouted. 'What what' she said. 'It's come off,' I said in despair. She was fully awake and sprang out of bed in a second, 'get into your chair, get into your chair.' It was easier going down than it was getting up. She pulled the soaking bottom sheet off. The under blanket was just as wet. There was another, not so bad, and another, quite a lot less. Mercifully, the last, just a little wet, she pulled off slowly. We both anxiously peered at the mattress, thank God it was dry. She threw more logs on the dying embers. There was a pair of bellows standing next to the fireplace. I started pumping while she collected the sheet and all the blankets and rushed into the bathroom. The fire began to catch. When there were a few inches of water in the bottom of the bath, she dipped the urine soaked circles into the water to rinse the hateful stuff out. All I could do was wring them out as hard as I could. She meanwhile ran back to the bedroom, collected all the chairs around the room, and put them apart but back-to-back, in front of the fire. I hadn't noticed how many chairs there were, why were there so many? I put more logs on the fire and blew it up furiously. She then hung the sheet and blankets between each couple of back-to-back chairs. This military style exercise was carried out with practised precision, with hardly a word between us. The room was so hot that sweat dampened our brows. She lay flat out on the mattress, so elegant, her skin glowing soft biscuit brown in the firelight. I wheeled slowly, forlorn, head down, back into the bathroom to stick on a new condom to my flaccid deflated penis.

It was an hour or two before the blankets were dry enough to make the bed up again. We were thankfully in-between lovely warm sheets just before a little knock at the door, where a cheery little housekeeper stood, with a tray of tea and biscuits.

We were so pleased she'd come; it was thirsty work drying blankets. In the broadest Scottish accent you can imagine she said, 'I hope you had a lovely night, everyone loves this room.'

THAT is an "accident", and I haven't started to tell you about the other awful problems of incontinence.

We had a lovely few days in the castle, being driven about the estate by the Factor; it was simply beautiful. One of the days the Laird suggested, as it was such a bright, clear, sunny day, would we like him to take us to the river Tay, which ran through the Estate. He'd show me where my wife, as a little girl and teenager, was rowed out into the middle by the gillie and caught all those magnificent fish. This was said with a wry chuckle as I think he knew very well; she hated fishing. Always cold, and very sorry for the fish, even if she only got a wee nibble. But the main purpose of the exercise was, for him, to push me in my wheelchair to the river, it was only about half a mile. So off we set at a fine pace with great gusto. The track had a high grassy middle which we managed to stay on most of the time despite our disabilities. Remarkably, he pointed things out as we went along and stopped exactly where the gillie would have rowed his boat to pick up his reluctant passenger. They'd travel either upstream or downstream, depending on where she'd get the best bites that day.

The wonderful stay came to a swift close all too soon, and we were in the courtyard saying our very fond farewells. We waved our unseen goodbye, to this brave and remarkable man, not knowing we'd never see The Laird again.

The level of kindness and sheer selflessness I have received from practically everyone I've come in contact with, over all these years, is extraordinary. But still I often find myself, when daydreaming, taking my mind back to that moment of knowing what was happening, and oblivion. If I had died, it all would have been so much easier. Yes, a shock for all concerned, but everyone would have got over it in a year or two. My wife would have remarried, my siblings would say, 'Yes, we used to have a brother, he died some time ago, a passenger in a car crash.' Instead, so many people have been tied to me and my illness for 39 years so far and will continue to be so, for probably, another 15 years.

Like most people I haven't achieved anything, I have no talent, I serve no purpose, why on earth go on and on and on. Is an individual life really that important, when millions of new ones are made so easily every day, and millions are destroyed every day? What is the importance of an individual without anything to offer? Perhaps this is where faith is a factor. I just cannot believe 'God' is anything other than a useful story. To me it's a children's story, made up to help people come to terms with difficult times in their lives, or for a meaning, or for a purpose in life at all. There's such an intriguing diversity in nature it's no wonder, before Charles Darwin's 'On the Origin of Species', the simple conclusion to nature's magnificence and Homo Sapiens immense power of thought, was that there is a loving God who must be worshiped. The Hindus have lesser gods, animals they're afraid of or are more powerful, to carry the message, whatever it may be, to the higher god. The Muslims have Mohammed, and the Christians have gone one step further and created the idea of the 'son' of God. But these are all stories, ones that should be put aside as we grow up. Unfortunately, they've all become big, big business and have caused the greatest misery and strife, for millions of people, for thousands of years.

Hello Babe

I was six weeks in Nairobi hospital on a special type of bed called a Stryker bed which turned me from my front to my back every two hours to avoid pressure sores. My Brother-in-law, a stockbroker on the London stock market, found it amusing I was being turned over every two hours as that's what brokers do to generate extra fees! So he bought my mother a few very cheap shares, on the New York exchange, in a small medical company called Stryker. In a few years those shares were to become so valuable they kept my mother in relative comfort for the rest of her life.

I don't quite know how I got from the crash site to the hospital where my wife eventually found me. It was a little African hospital in the town of Nyahururu with two of us in most of the beds. I awoke and looked straight into the eyes of an old African in an army greatcoat, carrying a paraffin lantern. He said to me in Swahili, that I had a severe wound on my leg and he was going to sew it up. I looked down, and indeed there was a nasty wound, a gash opening up to the bone, on the knee and right down the side of my leg. He had a huge needle and thread and proceeded to sew. It occurred to me I should be feeling a modicum of pain, so I assumed he'd injected a local anaesthetic, but there was no sign of any cleaning bowl or syringe. I drifted off. I awoke again looking into the face of another younger African in a white uniform. He spoke to me in English, 'You have broken your back, and you will never walk again.' I asked, 'Is my wife here?' He said, 'No, she doesn't know where you are, but we are trying to contact her.' I drifted off. I awoke again and looked straight into my wife's face. The feeling of relief was so intense, it took my breath away. I said 'Hello Babe, I've broken my back, and I'll never walk again.' She turned away aghast. The African nurse with her said, 'Be calm Mrs. Mayers he will be perfectly alright.' My wife later told me, she ran to the loo, getting there just in time before the total contents of her bowels emptied themselves. If that nurse could see me now, in our beautiful converted barn. Sitting at the kitchen table, looking out on to a lovely, sumptuous courtyard garden, she'd have the right to say, 'I told you so.'

But that would be after years of devastating trauma yet ahead. I'm sure Africans generally cope with disasters much better than we do here in the first world as they live so close to it, in their everyday lives.

Somehow it was arranged by my wife and our great friends Jill and Renaldo, for Peter and Jo, with whom we'd stayed so often, after delicious suppers and too much red wine, to come at daybreak. Driving the 100 miles from Nairobi to Nyahururu to collect me. We then made the long slow journey to Nairobi hospital, with me lying flat on a door and drugged to the eyeballs, in the back of Peter's Range Rover.It seemed an eternity for my poor little wife crouched in the back, but I was 'out-of-it'. Later I asked her how she'd found me, and what happened to the car.

Earlier that evening she'd had a faint, faraway telephone call, from a man with a strong, almost unintelligible Kenyan accent, briefly shouting down the line, 'Mr. Mayers has been involved in an accident, he is in hospital. Then the line went dead. She had no idea to whom she was speaking or to which hospital he was referring. All she knew was where I was headed that afternoon so I might have been in Nakuru hospital, where I was born, or I might have been in Nyahururu Hospital. They were sixty miles apart.

My Parents were away on a much-needed, long-awaited holiday in England, so we were living in the family home, my wife running my mother's business of Maasai Dancers. Busloads of tourists, from all over the world, would pour down the side of the valley every afternoon, to watch a troop of Maasai Moran (young warriors) performing their tribal dances.Then the tourists had an English tea with scones and cake, on the green, soft expansive lawn. To help her, living in the annex, she had a lovely young blond English girl, on her gap year, called Fiona. Fiona could never, ever have imagined the drama in which she was about to be involved.

My wife and Fiona set off into the darkness not knowing where they were going. After about two hours driving, they stopped at the turning to Nyahururu. Should they go on to Nakuru, or turn off to Nyahururu. By now my wife was beginning to panic. She took the turning to the latter. It was after midnight when they crept into the small, dirty, pitch-black darkness of Nyahururu. They stopped, not having a clue where to go. Out of the dense blackness, into the beams of the car headlights, emerged two young African men. She knew she was taking a risk, but she had no alternative. She wound down her window a few inches and as they passed asked in Swahili, could they please tell her the way to the hospital. They started to explain while coming towards the car. They bent down to look in. On seeing two girls by themselves, they both made a grab for the door handles trying to get in. My wife had the presence of mind to have already engaged the car in first gear. She surged forward, the two of them running after the car. Quite by chance, not far ahead, hardly daring to slow down, they spotted a small sign pointing to the hospital. The relief was short lived, as you now know what she was about to encounter.

It must have been around 2 am when there was nothing else to be heard, nothing else to be told and nothing else to be done. They were overcome with tiredness, but there was nowhere to go. The hospital had no spare beds. They remained sitting beside my bed in upright hospital chairs trying to get through the night. In the morning, my wife came with me, in Peter's Range Rover and Fiona drove the car back to the farm.

The everyday routine of hospital life quickly took over. Rolled from my front to my back, and stretched-out, with weights under my chin, and pulled by the ankles in the vain hope the spinal cord would have space for healing. Our friend Jill ran a little nursery school in Karen, an area named after Karen Blixen, who wrote 'Out of Africa'. During a painting class she asked all the children to paint pictures for a dear friend of hers who was in hospital and needed cheering up. She arrived the following afternoon with piles of paintings which she proceeded to stick on all the walls and on the ceiling. One very complicated one on the floor, which

I could analyse while rolled on my front. I'm sure this sort of therapy could be very therapeutic for anyone in my situation. Just by chance, and not that I knew at the time, one of those pictures was painted by a tiny tot called Natasha Kaplinski. Years later this close friend was staying with us in our barn in England. While idly watching the news one day, she said with utter amazement, 'Natasha Kaplinski, how on earth can that be?'

Meantime, my poor little wife was having a harrowing time. She was with me every waking hour, and being ferried back and forth to Peter and Jo's house, by kind, gentle, caring friends. Jo was waiting each night ready with a warm drink and a sleeping pill.

Kind, caring, gentle Fiona, slept in the next bed, to be with her when she suddenly awoke with crowding fears of unknown things to come. As far as my wife was concerned our life had ended. What on earth would we do now? Was it feasible to stay in Kenya? What would we do in England? The structure of our life had fallen apart. To add to this catastrophe, she had a telephone call from her brother to say her father had just died from colon cancer. The only way of coping with a horrific set of circumstances such as this is to think short term. Broken back? Stoke Mandeville. How to get there? Waiting list? Yes, of course. My Brother-in-law, in Kenya, was a doctor and had qualified with a friend who was at present at Roehampton Hospital in Richmond outside London. They were famous for treating the limbless but had less experience with paraplegia, but accepted me to see how I'd get on. I didn't get on very well, but it was while there, at Roehampton, we had an enormous change in our fortune. We met a woman called Marriott White.

Marriott's husband was paraplegic and had recently died. Her house in Notting Hill Gate was converted for him. So instead of moving, she decided to let it to people in wheelchairs from abroad. Talk about fitting the bill! We went for the weekend and stayed with her for five years.

I did go to Stoke Mandeville Hospital for five months, and what I was taught there was invaluable. I'll expand upon that episode later.

Bangalore

It was when living with Marriott we decided to go back to Kenya for a while, to be with my parents. It was on this first visit after the accident a friend came rushing to our valley with a book she desperately wanted us to read. It was supposedly a true account of 'miracles' being performed by an Indian Guru called Satya Sai Baba. He had a group of devotees in Nairobi, who were quite adamant that he did perform miracles, raising from the dead was documented, so making someone walk again, would be a doddle.

They helped us with all the contacts we'd need, and we were on our way to the Ashram in Bangalore in the next few days. There've been so many accounts and documentaries about India, you feel there'd be nothing new to say, but being there is quite different. There's never any quiet, you feel as though you're within a cauldron of people. The only peaceful things are the cows standing in the middle of the road. The cars never stop hooting, and they rush everywhere as though they'll be late for the next stop. Our contact in Bangalore was a dizzy Princess called Princess Devi. She was also a faithful devotee of Sai Baba.

The Ashram was relatively quiet and very well organised around the daily appearance of the man himself. The quadrangle he'd wander through was maybe a couple of acres, and the sea of people was divided into perfect squares by newly picked paths of bougainvillea petals. They were so thickly laid; his bare feet didn't touch the bare earth. The men and women were in separate squares, all sitting cross-legged, and all bowed as he slowly passed through us. Every now and again he'd stop, put his hand out, palm down, over a fortunate favoured one. He would move it slowly in a circle and ash would fall out, into eager stretched out hands, and be eaten there and then.

After some time of making the same exhausting, ritualistic journey every morning from the centre of Bangalore to Whitefields, the home of the Ashram, our Princess managed to elbow herself into a position on the edge of one of the squares, along a petalled path. So when the 'Great Man' happened to pass by, she threw herself in front of him and begged for an audience. He gave a small nod to a minion who contacted her later, and a privileged date was arranged. Much celebration ensued over the next few days. Parties were held at the Princess's palace, a little cottage on the edge of her father's little garden. Who was I going to give my wheelchair to when we left Bangalore? It would be a privilege for anyone else to sit in it. The state of elation really was quite infectious. Finally, the great day was upon us. Her father, the Maharaja, well, the brother of a deceased Maharaja, was persuaded to drive us himself, in his poor tired old Mercedes that had seen many a better day, to the meeting.

The inner gates to the sanctum were solemnly opened by two devotees, dressed in the ubiquitous white cotton uniform, with praying hands together and a little bow, as we slowly swept by. Other 'devotees' greeted us at every turn, with praying hands together and a little bow, and finally entered a small anti-chamber with a dozen plastic chairs facing a gold painted armchair on a dais. After a few minutes of silence and nervously exchanged glances, the door opened and the little man appeared. He was no more than five foot four, with a long afro hairdo that formed a black halo around his head, and a smiling friendly face. He was dressed in a bright orange floor-length gown. He wandered in and tucked himself into the gold armchair. Our Princess was on her knees speaking to him in Hindi. He looked at me and threw me a gunmetal medal with his name on it, one of the many abilities attributed to him was to materialise all sorts of things there and then. There was a gasp from the Princess. He then added, 'Complete cure.' Our Princess couldn't contain herself; she prostrated herself, full length on the floor in front of him. He then turned to my wife, and as a throwaway line said, 'You are a wonderful woman and you will have a son.' The Princess was overwhelmed. She screeched for joy, tears pouring down her cheeks. The audience was over; he gave us a little grin and left the room. The Maharaja drove us back to Bangalore.

What on earth do we do now? We'd waited six weeks for this news. Do we wait for the miracle to happen; having a son wasn't something I'd bargained for. No, no, just go home and rejoice; if he said it would happen, it would happen. So we did; go home that is. The Maharaja suggested, as we had to change our flight at Bombay, we could stay a night at the famous Taj Mahal Hotel. He'd give a little nod in the right direction, as an introduction. True to his word we found ourselves in a beautiful suite in the original part of the hotel. Incredible.

That six weeks in India, especially having never been there before, was the most extraordinary experience we've ever had. Needless to say, thirty years later, we're still waiting for the promises. Did we really believe I would walk again? No, of course not. So why did we go? We went solely because of peer pressure. There are many people, even within my own family and close friends, who'd have said to one another, 'He was offered a chance to walk again, but he chose not to take it.'

By some extraordinary misguided belief system, we were persuaded, by the same people, to go again. Can you believe it? Because Sai Baba's birthday is the same as mine, it was considered some sort of great significant omen. We were tied together. Only by being there, with him, in the village of his birth, on his birthday, would we know what he actually meant. So this time we made the long, seemingly endless journey, with our new dear, dear friend Marriott, with whom we were now living.

It was a hundred-mile drive from Bangalore, the road was appalling; dodging enormous potholes, missing oncoming vehicles by a whisker, and weaving between broken down trucks every few hundred yards. On arrival we were deposited in a completely bare concrete box, in a block of concrete boxes. It was on the third floor, no lift, and a cold water tap next to the squatting hole in the corner. The remote, tiny village of Puttaparthi is somewhere in the hills of South Central India.

I wheeled out of the box into the communal passage and looked down on to an incredible sight. From the edge of our building was a sea of bright, bright, colourful saris milling slowly about, tent after tent, marquee after marquee. In the middle of the huge, tightly packed square, with a range of blue hills in the distance, was a gleaming white house, ornately decorated, in what could only be described as baroque. Two huge domes with gold pinnacles, all built by the faithful devotees of the man we'd come all this way to see.

We'd been allocated a nice, white-suited student to push me about, and lift me up and down the three stories of our concrete block. We had one little room, about 12x12 to sleep in and the other small room was the squatting room with a cold water tap for ablution. There was nothing at all in the sleeping room. We three lined ourselves up on the concrete floor and there we were for about four nights.

Through the student, we asked if it might be possible to put in a request to be allowed another audience with the great man. The request was duly forwarded, but we were warned there were three thousand people ahead of us.

The time we were there, and the reason we were there, became for me, a blur, rather like being at school again. I wanted the whole thing to end. I didn't mean just this to end, I meant everything to end. But the whole of this event, culminated with the great celebration of our birthday, his and mine, and of course, the whole reason we were there.

The day was suddenly upon us and the Great Hall, where he'd be making his special appearance, began to fill, pack, would be more appropriate. In one section were the wheelchairs, hundreds of wheelchairs. I've never seen so many wheelchairs in one place ever again. Would it be possible they'd all had the same promise; and how many shared our birthday I'd like to know.

Once we were packed to the gunnels, as for a true superstar, we waited and waited, and waited. Why do they do that? He only had a hundred yards to walk from his white domed house. When he finally made his entrance, it was so undramatic. He slowly walked in from the very back of the hall, through the middle of us all. It didn't seem to be expected. Apart from us in wheelchairs, everyone else was seated cross-legged on the ground facing the stage. He stood there, at the back, patiently waiting for people to be aware of his presence, a little half smile on his face. As the people nearest him made double takes, they either stretched out their hands for his holy ash or bowed their heads to the ground. By the time he reached the stage the applause was shattering. He just stood there, with his half smile, in his floor-length bright orange silk gown, his arms hanging down, hands crossed in front, waiting. When the applause started to die down, he turned and walked slowly to the side of the stage to an ornate garden swing chair. The sort of thing you'd see in B&Q for £99.99 on pensioners' day. He didn't say anything, he didn't do anything, he just lay back on the swing chair swinging back and forth, smiling at us. I couldn't think what on earth was going to happen, surely something would happen, after all, this was the whole reason we'd come all this way. I turned to look at my fellow devotees for some indication. Nothing was forthcoming. They were all gazing at him with beatific smiles on their faces. Nothing else did happen. After quite a long time of smiling and smiling and swinging and more swinging, he stood up to further tremendous applause. He moved to the centre of the stage then walked slowly down through the middle of the hall and wandered out the way he'd come in. Was that it? That can't be it. I must have missed something. I must have fallen asleep. The whole hall started to fill with excited chatter. An elderly woman in a wheelchair next to me leant close and said in a hushed, conspiratorial voice, 'Vasn't that vonderful.' I said, 'It vas vasn't it.'

The following morning we started our long, long journey back to Bangalore, Mumbai and London.

The rent we paid for our little converted house was one case of Beaujolais wine a week. Most evenings our amazing friend invited us through to her adjoining house for supper, always accompanied by a couple of bottles of Beaujolais. This little house, with Marriot just a sliding door away, was our haven for five years. I'm not quite sure how everything we did over those years fitted together. We were lost. How my poor little wife put up with me, I really don't know. I was constantly ill with urinary tract infections, I couldn't eat, I was in constant, burning, exhausting pain and every morning I retched and retched before having a bath and getting dressed.

However ill someone is, however much they're suffering, a companion can't be expected to be with them 24 hours a day, 7 days a week, for years on end, with no prospect of any change. Yet my wife was always with me, she looked after me in every respect for all that time. She wasn't offered any help nor did she ask for any help. However, over the next thirty years we completed two huge building projects. Converting a burnt-out warehouse on the river Thames in London into three flats and a roof garden, and converting a disused old barn into a beautiful house for which we received a Sunday Times Award. We planted and ran our own 12-acre vineyard, and we travelled again to India, Rajasthan this time, then the Far East, Malaysia, Hong Kong, Singapore and Thailand. In Australia, starting in Western Australia, Perth, the train took us across the Nullarbor plain to Adelaide, a campervan from Adelaide to Melbourne and on to Sydney. A little aeroplane flew us from Sydney to Tenterfield in Southern Queensland for Christmas with dear relatives, then it was on to Cairns where my grandfather made his fortune in sugar. He left in 1918 to go, with his whole family of eleven children, to do the same thing in East Africa, Kenya where this agonising tale starts. We then completed our journey across the Pacific to Los Angeles, San Francisco, New York and back to London. We'd also been back some times to stay with my poor mother in our beautiful Kedong Valley. We've been to so many different places since my paraplegia I can't put them in order. Each place is a separate little story, with a beginning and end, its own entity.

Such Unkindness - Blessed Oceans

One awful entity was when my wonderful little wife was found to have breast cancer. To be told you have cancer must be bad enough, but for a woman to be told she has breast cancer, I can only equate with myself being told I would never walk again. Perhaps all husbands think their wives breasts are beautiful but my wife's breasts really are beautiful; the only way I can accurately describe them without being too overt is 'Page Three.' And now she was being asked to accept, what I can only describe as, mutilation. The cancer was a DCIS, ductal carcinoma in situ, which means it can't be removed without removing the whole breast, as the cancer is within the milk ducts. The surgeon told us he could build a reconstruction at the same time. He gave us the implant to hold and he said he could match the 'fall' of the other breast, but he couldn't save the nipple as the ducts there would also be carcinogenic. My little wife felt it was imperative she woke up with two breasts.

At this stage, as my wife figures so completely entwined in our lives together, I think I should paint you a picture of how she really is. When I refer to her as 'My poor little wife', I give you the wrong impression. It's a term of endearment I use to give you the sense of how I feel towards her. How I think I 'am' imposing upon her, how I 'hate' myself for being as I am. You might think she's a small, meek and put-upon person. She is neither meek nor small, and I don't think she'd ever describe herself as 'put upon'. She is a tall, strong, buxom, beautiful Englishwoman with a commanding presence. Her eyes are deep, deep brown with the whites of her eyes showing all around the iris. The irises are so brown they merge into the pupils, giving them a dense depth in which you could get lost forever. Her dark brown eyebrows are set well apart and emphasise her strong features. Her shoulders are broad and strong and her rounded, plump, beautiful breasts have the perfect fall. Her figure is hourglass and her skin is all a soft, pale biscuit colour giving her a natural glow.

She was admitted to the Royal Marsden Hospital in London to have a single mastectomy and reconstruction. She spent a week in hospital, I was with her all day, every day, and although, in great discomfort, all was going to plan. A couple of days after she was discharged, just before her first follow-up appointment, she began to feel unwell, a fever, and yes, the reconstruction had become infected. The whole thing had to be done all over again.

This time, we very nervously wove our way through the next five years of regular checks, when she was finally considered 'cured.'

Although the new breast was nothing like her own breast, we began to relax, and the whole dreadful episode slowly receded into the background of our everyday thinking.

The new breast had a valve on the side underneath the armpit, which meant the size could be adjusted after the effects of surgery had subsided. When my little wife, after about ten years, became aware of a small lump around the implant, we both felt it was probably the implant showing its age, and needing to be replaced.

If only it were that simple. Not only was the lump cancerous, a CT scan revealed it had metastasized, spread through the lymph system and throughout her lungs. By now we were punch-drunk. We could only listen to the oncologists with their strategy of how they would endeavour to treat it.

The drug therapy she was given immediately has so far been very successful, and reduced the size of the tumours in her lungs from peas to pinpricks. She has a CT scan and ultrasound every four months to follow progress.

So, instead of just sitting at home, nervously waiting for results every four months, we made one of the best decisions we've ever made; to go on a four-month cruise right around the world. Our little ship was called the Saga Ruby. We fell in love with that little ship, its crew and all its passengers. We visited thirty-six different countries over one hundred and fifteen days. As far afield as Tahiti and Bora Bora in the South Pacific and Beijing in the winter in the North Pacific. We walked on the Great Wall of China; my Pusher pushing me along. We wheeled right through the Forbidden City, a sight no one could ever forget, we were driven all about Beijing in a London taxi. We were taken to a Chinese play, where we sat in the audience at our own table, with drinks and little eats, and the actors moved and sang in high staccato. Dramatic and really quite touching.

We were taken to the Temple of Heaven. It was on the way there we had an experience I will always cherish. It's difficult to explain how moving it was. Our London taxi was parked on the edge of one of the few Beijing City parks through which we had to wheel to get to the Temple of Heaven itself. At the bottom of the long flight of steps up, was a large, open-sided, old stone courtyard, with covered stone passages along the sides. It was along these passages that like-minded, elderly Chinese would gather in the late afternoon, in groups of people with similar interests. Playing cards, playing chess, mahjong, discussion, singing, opera or operetta, men and women, all muffled up against the cold. We wandered slowly through them, from group to group, watching or taking photographs. No one took any notice of us; we might as well have been invisible. It wasn't a performance, it was just what they did, every evening, it was beautiful, and I'll never forget it.

At the end of a very long and intriguing, memorable day, we were taken to the most sumptuous hotel imaginable. Then at six o'clock in the morning the following day, without time to enjoy the lovely hotel, we were driven back the hundred miles, to our beautiful ship. Our butler was waiting for us at the cabin door and said, 'Welcome home.'

***

Another time, a long time before we found our lovely ship, a long time before beginning to find our way again, or even thinking there might be a way again. We were sitting on a blindingly white shimmering beach, overlooking the Indian Ocean, on the Kenyan coast, about a hundred miles south of Mombasa. The tide was at its lowest, you could smell the damp sand and the wet seaweed, and in the distance you could hear the line of white surf crashing on exposed coral reef.

I was in my wheelchair, my wife was on one side and a great friend, whom I'd been at preparatory school with years before, was on the other. He said, 'Let's go for a swim.' I said, 'That'll be great when the tide comes in.' He said, 'No now.' Before I could answer he picked me up in his arms and ran into the shallow water. Instead of putting me down in one of the hundreds of knee-deep little pools, he went on running. My little wife was running behind, she couldn't keep up. We clambered on to the exposed reef. Even Gwynne's knees began to buckle. He charged through the white surf and quickly into the deep blue water. I floated out of his arms, and immediately I could sense the immensity of the Indian Ocean. My legs had already been affected by osteoporosis so it wasn't possible for me to sink. I floated about on my back, stretched my arms up over my head, weightless, I turned over and looked down. I hadn't got goggles on so everything was very blurry, but I could see the reef wall plunge down out of sight. It was stunningly beautiful, little fish darting in and out of the colourful coral. I've always been able to hold my breath for a long time so I just hung there looking down, buffeted about by the small waves on the surface. I felt completely at peace. I wasn't aware of any pain. My body was absorbing energy. I didn't want to take a breath. I wanted to be part of this lovely enticing picture. I don't know how close I was to that moment, that millisecond before the oblivion of the crash. It would be so easy to end this awful struggle we were both yearning to be through. I rolled onto my back and took a deep breath. That experience was a pivotal point in my recovery. In the deep misery we were both suffering, I'd forgotten how much I loved the sea.

Stoke Mandeville

In retrospect, I began to realise it was while at Stoke Mandeville Hospital, I lost my will to live. By the time I arrived, I'd been six weeks in Nairobi Hospital, four weeks in St. Mary's Roehampton and one week with Marriott. No one could possibly have known, going to Stoke Mandeville Hospital, the star of stars for paraplegic rehabilitation, would break my spirit for years to come.

One of the most important things a paraplegic must learn is how to deal with double incontinence. I've explained earlier how I was taught to deal with urine collection and how unsatisfactory it was. So this is some sort of explanation for the far greater difficulty of dealing with the bowels. It's not a subject I really want to dwell on, but if I'm to tell my story at all truthfully, I must explain how awful and how curtailing the lack of bowel control really is. I've never seen it explained. Possibly for the same reason I'm reticent to do so now.

It's all very different now, but when I went to Stoke Mandeville Hospital, the present hospital was a far-off dream. So on arrival I was put into the dreaded 1X Ward, ruled with a rod of iron by Sister Rose. Sister Rose didn't put up with wimps, this was the situation, put up with it and deal with it. She was married to a man who could only move his head. And yet every morning he was up and dressed, bright and breezy, in his electric wheelchair, which he controlled with his chin, visiting people who were down in the dumps. Now, in the modern new hospital, the mattresses patients lie on have little motors to blow them up. This moves the air from place to place, making a ripple effect up and down the body, all to prevent the curse of pressure sores. But in those days we were laid out on four sets of two plump pillows, along the length of the bed. Every two hours, two orderlies and one nurse would come to the bed, the two orderlies picked me up flat in their arms while the nurse turned the pillows over and plumped them up. Then they would lay me down again on my opposite side. The whole ward of thirty beds had to have this procedure performed every two hours, night and day.

Although I was paralysed from the waist down, I couldn't move my top half at all. I couldn't sit up, I couldn't roll over, all I could do was move my arms and my head. This was understood at Stoke but not at Roehampton where dealing with defecation and urination hadn't even been touched upon. So as soon as the turning procedure was done, along came an orderly with a little tray on wheels, who said, 'How you feel today, fifty percent?' I smiled wryly. 'I'm going to plumb you up.' I just looked at him, it wasn't an expression I'd associated with myself. He pulled the sheet down, I was naked. He put on a pair of rubber gloves. He took hold of the end of my penis, pulled it straight up in the air and washed it, and my testicles, with a wad of cotton wool and disinfectant. He lay it down on a piece of paper from a roll. Then he opened a little jar which had a brush on the inside of the lid. On the brush was a thick white substance which he proceeded to paint along the length of my upheld penis I said, 'What's that?' He said, 'Glue.' I said, 'Glue?' He said, 'Yes, glue.' He took care to paint all the skin without any gaps. He then lay it back on the paper, he opened a little flat packet, and out fell what I thought looked like a condom. I said 'What's that?' He said, 'A condom.' I said, 'A condom?' He said, 'Yes, a condom.' I thought, 'I'm going to have to stop asking questions.' He then opened another little packet and out fell what looked like a small hard white plastic valve open at each end. He pushed that on the inside of the unrolled condom, then he picked up a short piece of rubber tubing, about six inches long. This he pushed over the hard white plastic valve, with the condom over it, fixing the tube, the valve and condom together. He then pulled my sticky white penis up, as long as he could, with the condom rolled over the head, then carefully rolled the rest of the condom down the length, covering all the glue. He squeezed it gently to make sure there were no air gaps. He then withdrew an ordinary sewing needle from a pincushion on the tray and carefully pushed it through the rubber tubing just above the hard white valve, to break the condom which had been pulled tight inside. He then attached the other end of the rubber tube to a long clear plastic tube with a litre bag on the end. He attached that to a wire holder which he hung on the frame of the bed. He then tapped my lower gut, just above the bladder, ten or twelve times, then pushed his fist, quite heavily into where he'd been tapping.The urine spurted out through this extraordinary collection of plumbing, and into the bag hanging on the side of the bed. He said, 'You must fill that,' pointing to the bag, 'twice a day.' He had a strong Moroccan accent, 'Now we teach you how to shit.'

Sister Rose's chocolate sauce caused a stench so foul, it cannot be matched anywhere on earth. My gut and everyone else's gut had to be emptied completely every second day, and the only place it could be emptied, was here, in this bed. It was emptied every second day to train it to be ready to empty itself when a suppository was shoved in by me, then empty itself while sitting on the loo.

All during this awful, dreadful time, my wonderful little wife was with me whenever she could be. Even when I was asleep in the day, after the torment of the chocolate sauce, I'd wake up and she'd be there. She was living in a B&B nearby, and her mother had lent her, her car. Her mother, who you would have thought would be aghast at her lovely daughter now tied to a cripple for goodness knows how long, was marvellous with her acceptance of the situation. I didn't deserve such kindness I was getting from all those around me.

After about ten days of enduring this torture, I was allocated a physiotherapist called Sally. She was a smiling, pretty, blond girl and very strong. We still correspond and see each other occasionally to this day.

To even get to the loo, and sit on the bloody thing, I first had to learn to sit up and not immediately fall flat on my face, or backwards, flat on the bed. Being paralysed from the waist is exactly like expecting a pencil to stay upright when letting it go with its point on the paper. This feeling of having no control was frightening and entirely unexpected. I really didn't think I was ever going to get it, other than holding on to something. All I had was the weight of my arms, if I was falling forward, I had to move my arms back, or if I was falling backwards, I had to move my arms forward. I suddenly got it. I can only equate it to finding you can ride a bicycle. You think your father is still holding you up, but he'd let you go at the other end of the drive.

The first 'go' at being on the loo was an absolute disaster. I managed to get into a wheelchair, sort of on my own, after quite a few lessons from Sally, but getting out of it and on to the loo seat, was beyond me. So the orderlies picked me up and put me there. The loo seat was a blow up one. As with most male paraplegics, the muscles on the buttocks quickly shrink away to nothing. Therefore the sacral bones can very quickly tear the skin from inside, it can take weeks of lying on your stomach to heal. They gave me my suppository and left me. I had a glove on the right-hand. I got my bearings and slowly tried to push the bloody thing up into the lower bowel, I couldn't get there without slightly leaning forward, With my left-hand I steadied myself by leaning on the front of the seat. I just got there and after some fumbling, not being able to find the anus, I shoved it up as far as I could. With relief, I leant back against the cistern, closed my eyes and waited for the result. Quite suddenly, without any warning, I lost my balance, my arms flailing all over the place, I crashed to the floor. I don't know how long I lay there, it seemed an age but it couldn't have been very long. The ward nurse came in to see how I was getting on, and said, 'What on earth are you doing down there.' She called the orderlies. The suppository had come out and lay, accusingly, on the ground next to me. They scraped me up and carried me back to bed, to fight another day.

The mornings started early to clear-up the dreadful results of the 'chocolate sauce'. I meanwhile had asked the ward nurse if I could stop taking it. She readily agreed. Apparently that's what they were waiting for me to do, not just me, everybody. It was part of the training process. As we were all so helpless, we'd naturally become reliant on the hospital and its system. They wanted us 'to question' and take back the responsibility of looking after ourselves; looking for potential sores; not staying in one position for too long; making our own decisions. Sally taught me how to handle my wheelchair. Get in and out of it from different heights, even from the floor and from the front. In and out of a high-sided bath, or a sunken bath. Even getting dressed had to be retaught. One thing had gone deep into my psyche. It was, of course, the chocolate sauce. Deep in the back of my mind, I'd resolved not to eat, nothing in, nothing out. Whenever mealtime came along, I felt sick and if I made myself eat, I retched and retched until it came up. Years later we talking about that episode with Sally, and she said, 'Yes, we thought we might lose you.' So when I said I'd like to leave, no wonder the request was so readily accepted!

One of the options we were given was to learn to use leg callipers, metal rods, hinged at the knee and strapped on with thick leather buckled belts, as a way of simulated walking. Practically all the paraplegics took up the offer. Obviously, if anyone had recently lost their ability to walk and then offered the chance to do so again, however clumsily, they would jump at the chance. The success rate was more or less 100% nil. The hospital knew this, but they had to offer it as an option because it was there. Sally wasted days and weeks, holding me upright, in one of the long, never-ending passages that seem to epitomise hospitals; She was trying to make a new method of walking with crutches and callipers instinctive. I'll try to explain it, see what you think.

You first buckle on the callipers, which are specially made for your legs. They must lock into the thick heels of a new pair of heavy leather walking shoes. Then you lock the callipers straight from the hinges at the knee. So with locked straight legs, and your hands holding the handles of the crutches, you place the points of the crutches, on the floor, right in line with the hubs of the large rear wheels of the wheelchair. Your upper arms are now parallel with the ground. You push directly downwards, with all your might, lifting yourself to a standing position so the soles of your new shoes are flat on the ground. Be very careful to keep your hips pushing forwards, to keep your upper body and legs in line. Don't look down, or you'll jackknife, and fall flat on your face. Stand there for a minute or two, to get your bearings. It's worth the effort just to see life from that viewpoint again. You'll wonder how on earth you're going to make your legs move forward, one by one, to start walking. Move the points of the crutches forwards, and place them about a shoe's length ahead of the shoes and lean on them. You can start with the right or left leg, so I'll start with the left. Move your weight on to the left crutch and use your upper body, on the left, to lift the left hip, raising the left shoe off the ground. It will then swing forward, ahead of the right leg, then let it drop to the ground by relaxing your upper body. You have taken your first step. Then shift your weight on to the right crutch, lifting the right leg with your upper body, allowing the right leg to swing past the left one, and so on, step after step. It's so easy, one step, then another step, away I went, you couldn't see me for dust... in my dreams.

All my dreams were so clear, so detailed, so distinct, like the beautiful animated cards you receive online on your birthday and Christmas, always about moving my legs. Sometimes, in a half-awake state, I felt my legs moving under the sheets, so I determined to keep them moving while I awoke fully, feeling they would go on moving when fully awake. It was very depressing when this happened, and then waking to be confronted with the stinking ward. Never once did I learn to take an unaided step.

Another incredible device I was told about while at Stoke Mandeville hospital, without which I really don't know how on earth I would have coped, is an internal/external bladder controller. As it was still regarded as 'experimental', it couldn't be entirely funded by National Health Service. But its implantation could be if I could fund the device itself. My Aunt Carmen offered to buy it for me. Such a kind offer I really didn't deserve. Internally, on the left side of my chest, under the skin, is implanted a signal receiver. Two wires are threaded down under the skin, around to my spine and down to the vertebra, thoracic number 12 to the nerve endings that control the bladder. By chance, the spinal cord was cut by the collapse of vertebra number 10. The control box is about the size of a packet of cigarettes. Externally, I hold its fellow receiver over the one under the skin. An electric shock, at a particular frequency generated by the little box, contorts the bladder for about 10 seconds. This automatically cuts off releasing the neck of the bladder, the sphincter muscle, allowing all the urine to shoot out and down the pipe to the bag on my leg.

Talking about electric shocks, it brings to mind another short interlude involving just that. I accepted my wife might like to have a child of her own one day. So we brought up the subject at one of my outpatient check-ups. I obviously needed to produce sperm, without the ability to have an erection and ejaculate. I really don't know if this is how it's done now, but we were told an electric shock had to be administered directly to the prostate gland. Can you imagine! Hopefully sperm might find its way out into an awaiting test tube. It would be taken immediately to the lab for analysis. This odd procedure took place and yes a small amount of sperm did dribble out and was hurriedly sent to the lab. Shortly the result returned, only to reveal there were a few sperm but they were all dead. I said, 'Of course they're dead you've just electrocuted the poor little buggers.'

New York and Colorado

We returned to Marriot's little haven, but we still had no idea what we were going to do. One day my Brother-in-law Douglas, my little wife's elder brother, of whom Marriot was very fond, breezily walked into our little house. He threw a newspaper on to my lap, and said, 'There you are, you can go and do that.' He'd circled an advert for the sale of a 2000 acre wheat ranch in the mountains of Colorado in America, for 2,000,000 dollars.

Just by chance, on a visit back to Stoke Mandeville, we'd met a flirty French girl called Anne-Marie, who'd also been paralysed in a car accident a few years before. Her boyfriend, a very wealthy Iranian I think, had said to us, 'If ever you think of something you'd like to do, that needs financing, I'll look into it if you like.' So I rang him. He said 'As it happens I'm going to San Francisco next week, so I'll fly to Colorado with my lawyer. We'll meet the agents and go and see the place, then take it from there.' True to his word, he did all that and when he came back, he said 'You must go and see it for yourself, because you'll have to run it.'

A relatively major problem we had was that we didn't have any money, other than the value of our house in Clapham, which was presently let. Well, not enough money, even for the flights there and back. So we flew from London to New York on stand-by. We couldn't book the flight back because you obviously can't book a stand-by. At Kennedy Airport we were met by the brother of a very dear friend in Kenya. He gave us the most outstanding few days in New York anyone could ever dream of having. So unexpected, out of the blue, and with no money.

Peter was a huge, all-enveloping character, full of merriment and a zest for living. Every part of every day was to be lived to the full. From the first cup of coffee in the morning to the last double vodka at midnight, whether at work or play, was to be packed with humorous activity, innovation and generosity. All this didn't exactly make for a peaceful existence, but for a visitor to New York, for the first time, it was the most exciting time anyone could ever wish for. We stayed with Peter for only about a week, but the amount we packed into that week made it seem more like a month. I'd always understood New York was a city like no other. How right it proved. 'New York never sleeps.' You could feel the thrum of that city, from the walls, on the pavements, high up in the sky, deep down in the basements, the whole city was alive. So it was very apt that, by profession, Peter was an indoor and outdoor garden designer. He ran his own little nursery right in the middle of the city, and when I wheeled into that small shop, we really did feel we were magically being pulled into another world. His three bubbling girls working for him were all slightly different. You couldn't put your finger on it, wacky, quirky, not 'off-the-wall' but nearly. Great fun to be with for a while, but living in 'Wonderland' I think would be too exhausting for the average person. I do wonder what happened to them, what would they be doing now? Peter took us to the early morning flower market, the famous fish market, the vegetable market, the unbelievable meat market. The sheer amount of food consumed by one city in one day, admittedly an extraordinary city, was for me, coming from East Africa, where all food is a precious commodity, somehow seemed to highlight the difference between the third world and the developed world. He took us to New York Central Station where we swallowed the biggest, juiciest oysters I'd ever tasted. Being inside a building like that, and watching all the thousands of people scurrying around all knowing where they were going, on the whole not bumping into each other, reminded me so much, of huge flocks of little birds. They glide about the evening sky, painting great patterns, shapes and waves before settling on their roosting trees or grasses. Apparently they do bump into each other when forming all those lovely arching waves, but it happens so quickly, we humans can't pick it up.

Peter took us to nightclubs high up in the sky, I'd always imagined nightclubs were in basements. Sitting at a table so high up, drinking an enormous dry martini, where all single helpings of food and drink were enough for six Africans, I temporally became quite overwhelmed, a sensation I don't remember having had before. Looking out over the city at midnight, was simply stunning, mesmeric.

This man-made view is now very similar to many modern cities; Hong Kong, Kuala Lumpur, Bahrain, Muscat, Shanghai and of course closer to home, Chicago and Detroit. However often I visit one, I never cease to marvel at the sheer engineering feat, the complexity of bringing together all the different trades we use every day, and now take for granted, to build these fantastical structures.

Peter, with his exuberant, imaginative personality was well suited to creating little garden havens throughout the city. Once he'd created a garden it had to be maintained, and as it grew it changed character, and so on. He had access to so many apartments he said he felt like Dick Whittington, being given keys to the city. He'd also built himself a most unusual, beautiful octagonal house, in the country about three hours north of New York. It was on a cliff top overlooking the forests of New England; you can imagine the spectacular golden rolling views in the Autumn. He had, of course, taken charge of the wheelchair for once, my little wife, who never takes her eye off me, ever, was able to relax in the knowledge, with his great strength, nothing untoward would happen to me.

But life is so cruel, a few years later Peter was diagnosed with cancer. After only a year, a man of such character, generosity and a love of life, and so many friends who loved him, was reduced to nothing. He died a bitter, miserable, agonising death in his beautiful home, looked after by his sisters.

The full, colourful, wonderful, joyful week flashed by, and so it was back to work, waiting in the standby queue to Colorado Springs, where we were met by two very baffled land agents. However, they were very polite and dutifully drove us to our motel for the night. The following day was to be the beginning of a very strange experience, from which we only just emerged by the skin of our teeth.

The highway dived south-west into the first range of the Rockies. Up and up we climbed, looking back over huge expansive blue mountains. The drive took about four hours, owing to the nationwide 50 mph speed limit in America at the time. We started to descend, ears popping, and soon, there, laid out before us, was a dead flat plain, edged all around in the far distance by a thin line of more blue mountains. In the centre of the picture, which somehow seemed familiar, was a small township consisting of a few shops either side of the highway, a petrol station and a motel. We stopped the car. All was silent. 'And there,' said the agent proudly, 'is Alamosa,' he paused, then said, 'And there, to the left, is your ranch.' We looked in silence. 'Gosh,' I said. I turned to look at my little wife. The look on her face was a mixture of horror and terror. She was speechless, motionless, her deep brown eyes staring at the scene in front of us. They began to fill with water. The agent awkwardly broke the silence, 'I guess we'd better check-in first, then we'll go see Jim.'

Jim Hunter was the owner of the ranch, and as luck would have it, the Mayor of Alamosa. The enormous production of wheat per acre relied upon vast quantities of water sprayed on to the crop, night and day, through boomed roundels, covering a hundred acres each. The water came from deep wells, or boreholes for which only he seemed to have the rights. We were taken to his house, a typical modern American house which also came with the property, and introduced to his wife. I asked for and was shown, the spreadsheets showing the enormous profitability, so we asked why they'd decided to sell. The wife's eyes filled with tears. It turned out, the previous winter when the whole plain was covered in deep snow, their son had crash-landed his small aeroplane when trying to land in front of the house and was killed.

The comprehensive meeting lasted about a couple of hours, then the Mayor suggested a tour of the ranch. This was man's business so the wives were left together to chat. The only thing of any note was a large metal hanger full of beautiful farm machinery. I love farm machinery, it takes me back to when I was a boy on my father's ranch. Inside the hanger were two enormous four-wheel drive tractors with air-conditioned cabs. Along the sides were all manner of attachments, ploughs, harrows, seed drillers. By now, the younger of the two agents had, completely unselfconsciously, taken charge of me and the chair, We stopped in front of two attachments I'd never seen before. They were quite simple, each had an enormous thick hook, more than 3-foot long. The Mayor said, in his broad southern drawl, 'See these, these are responsible for the enormous tonnage we get per acre. The whole plain has very deep topsoil, but it's packed like concrete. These hooks break it up. Then I put the ploughs in to turn it over, then the harrows. Then,' he paused for effect, 'I drill twice, first time deep, and the second just above the first.' He paused again, 'Double drilling, double tonnage.' The three of us just looked at him and nodded. It made sense, why hadn't anyone thought of it before. Maybe they had, but I'd never heard of it.

That evening we were taken by the agents to a motel in Alamosa where we'd spend the night. I went to the room to rest a bit. I was still retching and retching every morning and still felt sick at the thought of eating, so I got tired very quickly. I don't know why, but I felt I had to insist on buying supper for the two agents. I suppose it must have been because I felt so insecure. My wife meanwhile, had gone to the shop attached to the motel where she had a very strange experience. While she was looking around, the little Chinese woman in charge, sidled up to her, and whispered, 'What are you doing here?' My wife was obviously a bit taken aback, she said, 'We're thinking of buying The Hunter Ranch. 'She looked shocked and very frightened and said, in a, fearful whisper, 'No, no you mustn't, you must go, he is a very bad man, we live in fear of our lives,' She scuttled away.

The following morning we were driven back to Colorado to meet the younger agent's family. I always had a very high regard for Americans, as they were the nicest, most outgoing groups of all the nationalities who came to visit us on the farm. But still I was surprised by their daughter who was no more than twelve. On hearing we were invited to a barbecue on Saturday said, 'You'll have a nice time, they're very charming people, so you'll have a lot in common.' Can you imagine an English girl of twelve saying that? Indeed, we did have a nice time and they were very charming. A couple of days later, after waiting for more stand-by flights, we were back with Marriott, shattered and wondering what on earth we'd done. I hadn't noticed my poor little wife had come out in a rash all over her body, with the awful prospect of going to live in Alamosa Colorado. I've asked her now why didn't she say anything at the time, and she says, 'I couldn't, you were suicidal.' She also says I wouldn't have understood her feelings, because all men are autistic, in just varying degrees.

A few weeks later, during negotiations with Jim Hunter, our backer, our financier, our whole reason for doing all this, suddenly died of a heart attack. All negotiations immediately ceased and my wife's rash disappeared overnight.

Africa

It wasn't until years later, when we found our beautiful little ship, the Saga Ruby, we were able to enjoy being 'on' the sea as opposed to being 'in' the sea. On occasion we were at sea for six days on the trot; it was these days that were of such special significance. The whole outside wall of our cabin was glass which slid open on to a balcony. I would sit there for hour after hour, drinking coffee and watching the sea. Suddenly a small school of flying fish would break the surface and wing their way ahead of the ship. Dolphins would come and play in the prow for ages, jumping over the waves. Such a beautiful, graceful freedom.

A couple of years after Gwynne dashed me out to the exposed reef and through the waves to let me float free in the beautiful immensity of the Indian Ocean, he himself was to suffer his own considerable trauma.

He was, by profession, a bush pilot, so it was that feeling of the need to be free, he understood so well, without having to explain or vocalise it in any way. He was working for a French company in Southern Sudan ferrying the workers back and forth from their camp on the border with Kenya to where they were building a huge canal, called the Jonglei Canal. Its purpose was to divert the White Nile away from its natural course through the Sudd swamp, and join it again about three hundred kilometres north; thereby increasing the water available for agriculture a hundredfold.

Although The Sudd can be looked upon as a nuisance, it is a vast ecosystem in its own right. The implications of depriving it of such a vast quantity of water so quickly surely can't have been thought through properly. It was the lack of thought, or sheer stupidity, that, arguably, gave the Southern Sudanese Freedom fighters the right to stop the canal being built. It was, for this reason, Gwynne, his pregnant wife, little son and fellow pilots were captured. Apart from his wife and child, who later had to be abandoned to be found by the following army, the others were held hostage in the bush for more than a year. They only just survived by catching grubs and insects. The small amount of water they were given was filthy and stale. They were all very, very ill and at times close to death.

Finally, a ransom was negotiated and they were released. The reason why this episode in Gwynne's life comes into my story is because, just before he was captured, he had spotted and bought a small, all-terrain vehicle. He thought it would be ideal for me. He could NOT have been more right. I have used that vehicle, and ones like it, to this very day. When I'm in it, I literally can go anywhere. It's very fast so I can speed along any beach at about thirty miles an hour. It can swim out to the reef at low tide. It floats, so deep pools make no difference. I can fly out through the tall grass on the savannah plains in amongst the herds of game. As long as I don't get too close they don't gallop away. They don't know what I am, so they just stand and stare. I can climb over huge boulders, I can pick my way through dense woods, or through forests of tall majestic oak trees or beach or pine. It's rather like an upturned bath only wider. It has six balloon tyres; three either side, all driven simultaneously by a small motorbike engine. It's steered by two levers that brake one side or the other. The only trouble with this one, my first one, is the engine would suddenly decide to stop, and nothing, nothing would persuade it to start again.

For some reason, best known to herself, my little wife, who looks after me as though I'm made of the thinnest porcelain imaginable, doesn't let me drive alone in the car. The buggy is another matter entirely. All she'd ask, 'Have you got enough petrol?' I'd say, 'Yes, and I'll be some time, I don't know how long.' That's all.

So it was on one occasion, I set out, on my own, down from the house in the Valley, on to the plains below. In those days the plains were full of all sorts of game, Thompson gazelle, Grant, Kongoni, Zebra, prancing Impala, all the plains game. Way, away I went,further and further; it was so beautiful; compelling. I stopped and turned off the engine. I was 'there', complete, listening to the silence. The sound of the soft breeze wafting gently through the tall brown succulent grass, the sweet smell of fresh hay, the munching of the animals all around. I felt part of the whole, I was part of nature.

I don't know how long I was there, but it must have been an hour or two. I began to think I should get back. I reluctantly turned the key to start the engine. It didn't take. I turned it again, still it didn't fire. I opened the choke; still nothing. I wasn't worried yet; I waited a bit, I tried again, nothing, again and again, still nothing. The battery started to show signs of strain. There was nothing I could do, I just sat there, I was marooned. What was I to do? I looked all around me in a different light; instead of the beauty I've just described, I saw nothing for miles around; there were no roads anywhere near, why would anyone come this way. I knew I'd eventually be missed, but where would they begin to look for me? I just sat in a stunned stupor. I stared ahead, empty of thought.

Then slowly in my gaze, on the horizon, there seemed to be a figure. I went on staring. It was a figure, it was a Maasai, his skin covered in red ochre, his hair braided with fat and ochre, falling to his shoulders. He was carrying his long sharp spear and wooden knobkerrie, his long knife in its red leather sheath around his waist. He stopped right in front of the buggy, threw the blunt end of the spear into the ground to lean on, he said, 'Sorba (hello).' I said 'Sorba.' He said, 'Habari (How are things).' I said in Swahili, 'I can't start my engine.' 'Ah,' he said and continued in Swahili, 'let me look.' I lifted the cover off the engine, we both bent over looking into it, like two men anywhere in the world, 'Ah,' he said again. He pulled his spear out of the ground, turned it around, and carefully threaded the long sharp blade down to a little screw on top of the carburettor. He gave it a small, gentle turn and said, 'Jarribu (try it).' I turned the key and the engine burst into life.

Without another word, he got into the buggy next to me and pointed with his spear where he wanted to go. After a little while we approached his Manyatta (a collection of rounded huts made of dung). A crowd of little children, all completely naked, poured out of all the huts, screaming with laughter, running to greet us. They were laughing so much they could hardly stand up. As the Moran stood up to get out, the children, still doubled up with laughter, formed an orderly little queue. They moved one by one, towards the Moran, bowed their little heads, while he gently laid the flat of his hand on each one. We shook arms goodbye, and amid gales of laughter, from jumping, waving, naked little black bodies, I sped off into the fast approaching gloom.

I was slightly worried about my reception. Dusk was just beginning to come down. I'd been away quite a long time. I drove into the parking area and up to my chair. I transferred out of the buggy, into the chair and gingerly pushed myself on to the veranda. Everyone was there, merrily chatting away. I got a warm greeting from all the family, and a kiss from My little wife, 'Hello, hello, have you had a lovely time?' 'I've had a wonderful time.'

This moment, and its reaction was very significant. It meant I was getting back my independence. No one was trying to take away my independence, but inevitably, I'd become mollycoddled and it was now up to me, to show I could stand on my own two feet, so to speak.

It must have been on this visit to my family in the Valley, we were driving into Nairobi when an incident took place with a traffic policeman. A new flyover had been built over our usual road, to relieve the incredible volume of traffic that had come about since we were last here. I made a stupid mistake and started to come down off the flyover into the oncoming traffic. Very quickly I realised the mistake and backed up, but two or three cars had to weave their way around me. Only a couple of minutes from joining the dual carriageway, a policeman stepped forward with his arm up in the air and the other vigorously waving me to the side. He was furious, 'What do you think you were doing?' he shouted in his thick Kenyan accent, 'You could have caused a grave accident,' 'I'm very sorry Officer, you see the last...' 'No, no, no, no,' he shouted waving his finger in my face.'Do not make excuses to me', then pointing to his badge on his cap, 'You have not got a leg to stand on.' I paused and said, 'Do you know Officer, you're absolutely right.' He stood back and puffed up, 'So... I am right.' 'Yes Officer, I'm very sorry, I shall never make that mistake again.' He paused and half shouted, 'OK, this time I will let you go, but if I ever have to stop you again, I will throw the book at you, now go.' I went.

Rotherhithe

I later reflected on what he'd said. He was right, of course, not only literally but in any other sense as well. I think this must have been about 1983, seven years after the accident. We were living in our beautiful warehouse in Rotherhithe, just below Tower Bridge in South-East London. So why did I still have this terrible sense of nothingness, pointlessness, uselessness. It's not as though we'd done nothing for seven years; and yet every morning I would wake up feeling sick; I would retch and retch until my stomach muscles ached. We'd borrowed a lot of money to convert the warehouse, but we paid it all back just by selling one floor, completely empty, twenty feet by sixty. In those days we still had bank managers. They would guide and advise and would look back through your financial record, and would let you extend your overdraft, as long as you let them know first. In this case he said, 'I expect you're going to have to do a lot of hard talking.' We both said, 'We think it'll speak for itself.' We picked him up in South Kensington, drove him over Tower Bridge, through all the huge derelict warehouses, to the Mayflower pub. The Mayflower ship did actually set sail to America from here, and our little warehouse nestled between two other monsters which soon would succumb to the developers. We pointed it out and he said, 'Oh I see,' and that was it. We drove him back to South Kensington.

When it was finally finished and friends came to visit, it had the same sort of effect as people had when they first saw Kedong. It took their breath away; at any time, day or night, the tide, in or out, people's jaws would drop.

I should tell you of the immensity of the task upon which we'd just embarked. The owner of the warehouse was a friend of Marriott's called Angelica Garnet, whose husband David wrote the book Aspects of Love, subsequently made famous by Andrew Lloyd-Webber's musical. She asked £45,000 which even then, in 1981, was an incredible, out-of-the-blue, opportunity, to save us from my overriding depth of worthlessness, of my life, not serving any purpose. There was no point in having a survey; the building was a burnt-out, London stock brick shell, with no roof. The thick brick walls were built sitting directly on the clay London is built on. It was probably built in about the 1850s when the London docks were at the peak of their worldwide trading network. But modern building regulations stipulate brick walls must sit on concrete or a similar material as a solid foundation. This seemed to me to be an impossible demand, least of all because the building had happily stood there, with no movement for more than a hundred years. But our very clever new friend and architect, Colin White, who lived opposite us in Marriott's mews, worked out an ingenious, relatively simple way to solve the problem. The clay had to be cut out in arches underneath the brick walls only two at a time, then the arches filled with concrete and allowed to set for a few days. This tiresome procedure was carried out until the whole building was sitting on the top of all the new concrete arches. The rest of the clay, between the arches, was then dug away and filled with concrete. The entire structure of about 100ft deep, 50ft wide and three stories high now sat comfortably, on its new foundation of 300 tons of spanking new concrete.

The design of the interior could now materialise. My wife has a natural eye for design and so has Colin. Two cooks in the kitchen is a recipe for conflict. But they managed to steer gingerly around each other for the next three years it took to create, and the outcome was spectacular.

We had all this and had done all I've described, and yet we were both on the edge. I can see clearly now why it was my poor little wife was in such despair. But then, when I found her curled up on the end of the sofa, sobbing her heart out, I said, 'What's the matter?'

I was so immersed, enveloped in my own deep misery at being cut in two, tied for the rest of my life to this primitive, cursed contraption of a wheelchair. I couldn't see the devastating effect

I was having on the people closest to me. I'd started to drink a bit too much whisky. After a very nice supper with a bottle of wine, we'd watch television, then maybe turn off all the lights and watch the nightlife on the river. My little wife would go to bed and I'd stay in the sitting room, with a glass of whisky, listening to very loud music on my headphones. On the very first night in the warehouse, having moved away from the womb of our wonderful Marriott's house in Notting Hill Gate; the vicar of Rotherhithe arrived, with a bottle of whisky, to welcome us to his Parish. He stayed and stayed and I happily drank and drank. When trying to transfer out of the wheelchair into bed, I collapsed on the floor and, without knowing, my leg snapped in two just below the knee. My exasperated but forbearing little wife, struggled, with all her might, to lift my deadweight back into the chair and on to the bed. It wasn't until the morning, when I pulled back the duvet, the sight of my massive, swollen leg, caught me unaware, causing me to almost pass out.

The ambulance drove me to A&E at St. Thomas' Hospital. There they decided to plate it together, rather than put me in plaster, because of the possibilities of pressure sores. The bane of a paraplegic's life. This whole procedure required a week's stay in the hospital.

It was not possible for my battered, bruised, and now desperate little wife to be completely alone for a week in that warehouse. There was no alternative but to retreat to the safety of Marriott's home in Notting Hill Gate.

Unfortunately we only lived at the warehouse for three years. I think it was during those three years I became aware that the agony I was going through was of my own making. If it was of my own making, why on earth would I want to put myself through this misery, this destruction.

Some time ago Marriott told me that my Brother-in-law had said, 'Of course, he is very selfish.' I disregarded that as something a brother-in-law might say as a dismissive remark about someone for whom he had no regard. However, it slowly dawned on me during the time we were at the warehouse, everyone around me had done their utmost to make me accept that life was worth living.

I explained earlier, soon after being paralysed, it was as plain as day to me I hadn't achieved anything, I had no talent, I had nothing to warrant any of the enormous love, care and attention that was being poured upon me. I was so engrossed in my own deep misery, I didn't realise the effect I was having on the people closest to me. It was in the nick of time the realisation flooded over me. For seven years I'd been creeping through a dark, wet, clammy, stinking tunnel without any reason to make me go forward. My head bowed, my face just above the mud I was hoping would drown me, when suddenly, without any warning, I looked up and I saw this magical scene all around me. The feeling was as though I'd stepped back in time to my childhood, into our beautiful garden I've described earlier. Everything was there. Why, why did I ever have to leave. Both my Parents were still alive, my Ayah was still alive, our beloved little pack of assorted four-legged super-friends were still with us. But now I had someone else who'd been with me while I'd been creeping through that dreadful tunnel, not caring, not knowing if I was going backwards or forwards. I didn't know she was always nudging me forwards

Quite recently, long after we left the warehouse, there was a story in the papers, of a young man who'd suffered exactly the same accident as me. He had decided, very early on, he would not live a life from a wheelchair because he could not accept the compromises he knew he'd have to make. He was told he'd get used to it, he was only eighteen and another world would open up. He said he didn't want to get used it and he was not interested in 'another world' opening up. Somehow he persuaded his parents to take him to Dignitas in Switzerland, where he would take his own life. I only recall that story as an example of the extremes people go through when presented with paraplegia as a way of life. Even now, after all this time, knowing all I know he'd have to go through, I can't honestly say he made the wrong decision. So here I was, without the option of going to Dignitas. I had to accept all the love and dedication so many people had given me over the last seven years and repay it by 'trying', just 'trying.' Nobody would ask for more.

***

During the time we lived with Marriott, another beautiful little character came into our lives; tiny in stature but with a huge personality. We both came from dog-owning families and while living in the Kedong valley, our great joy was our little pack. Five, wonderful, very different, assortment of the most beloved four-legged friends, only other dog owners would understand. When we had to leave Kenya, it was as if our hearts were being torn out of our bodies. So when this tiny ball of fluff was deposited on my pillow after Marriott and my wife came back from a shopping trip, there was nothing but instant love. She was a miniature Yorkshire terrier called, on her pedigree, Nonsense Lady Rotherhithe; without her I don't think my poor little Wife would have retained her sanity. She gave us fifteen years of pure love and utter delight. When she died, I thought my little wife's heart would break. Before witnessing what was happening to her, if you'd told me someone could die of a broken heart, I would have disagreed with you. But now, I know you can become very ill with devastating grief. Her body was racked with sobbing. Not just for one or two days but for weeks. She had an illness for which there was no consolation. There was no placating, no let-up. We say the love dogs have for their owners is unconditional. Now I know the love some owners have for their dogs, is also unconditional and total.

That little character was with us wherever we went. She'd even sit on my right arm, my accelerator and brake arm when we drove around London. She recognised places where she could go for a run. If we couldn't stop, she'd look back inquiringly. Because of her we became very close to my Uncle and Aunt who lived in East Sussex; they doted on her. So it was with them she stayed when we returned to Kenya to see my mother in the Kedong Valley. And it was because of her, they wanted us to live close to them. So it was because of her they found an old derelict barn in which we now live, and probably will do so for the rest of our lives.

Storm and Stuttgart

I find it difficult to place all the episodes I've talked about, in order of them happening. I can say though if they happened in a good time or a bad time. So from June the 29th. 1976 until the end of 1987 was a bad, bad time. There were lighter moments of course, but generally I was deeply depressed and couldn't really find any purpose in living. We did do things. By now we'd moved from our beautiful warehouse and into our derelict barn.It had been transformed into a magnificent four bedroom house with underfloor heating.It was set around a courtyard with raised beds so I could participate in the creation of a wonder. It was only my poor little wife who knew what was really going on. People would say to her 'He's amazing how he handles everything.' She wanted to throttle them. She knew it was only her who kept the 'show' on the road. She finally said to me, it was unfair, selfish and deeply wounding to continue with this attitude after everything she, and so many others had done their utmost to make my life worth living. She was right. It was now up to me. I was very lucky, people had put up with me for so long.

So it was 1987, the year of the great storm that swept into the South-East of England, tearing down great swaths of beautiful, mature forest and scattering them about like matchsticks. It was 1987, more than ten years after that accident I seriously began the long fight back to reality and fulfilment. I said to my wife, just the other day, 'how is it we now have so much when we had so little.' The answer is here with me now and has been all the time. How she waited all that time, I just don't know.

***

Soon after I was first paralysed, and still in the hospital in Nairobi, it was suggested, to My poor little wife that I should meet another paraplegic. He'd fallen off a horse and broken his back not long ago. He was permanently in a wheelchair, as would I be. I'm not quite sure why it was thought this meeting would raise our spirits. However, he wheeled himself along to my ward, every inch of wall space covered with Jill Retief's children's school water paintings and introduced himself. His name was Bill Argent. He was a cheery chap of about fifty. I don't know why he thought he was there, he had nothing of any hope to say to me, it was quite evident, that was that. Anyway, we both made an effort to chat and it turned out, before his accident, he was Managing Director of Mercedes-Benz Kenya and amazingly still was.

After eventual admittance to Stoke Mandeville Hospital, I found he was well remembered, 'as the man who never left his job'. Very unusual. He spent hours every morning on the telephone to his office in Nairobi, running the business from his hospital bed. He'd taken no time to adjust to an entirely new way of living. He didn't consider he had an illness, he might as well have broken his leg, so he only stayed in hospital the shortest possible time. That attitude might have been a useful tool for the short-term, but I'm afraid for the long-term, or even the medium to long-term, it was to cost him his life.

We chatted quite amiably about all sorts of things, other than what life was like living from a wheelchair. Later I was to realise, nobody ever talks candidly about living their life from a wheelchair. It's too intimate and awful to relate. Much of the awfulness is centred around incontinence, the 'telling' of which, makes normal people uncomfortable. So switch off now, if you don't what to hear any more!

We came back to our beautiful Kedong Valley, almost a year later. Among the many friends we had to see again, who'd been so wonderful to us during the time I was in hospital, was to contact Bill to see how he was getting on. All the dreadful difficulties I now knew so much about had begun to crowd in, but with his strength of character he coped and somehow managed to continue working. On one of our visits, after extolling the design and abilities of Mercedes-Benz engineering, he suggested it would be possible for him to organise a car to be built for me personally. If I could collect it myself from the factory in Stuttgart, there'd be no duty to pay, so the overall cost would be as affordable as most other well built cars. We'd never entertained the idea of having a Mercedes, they'd always been far out of our reach. My father had bought us a second-hand Peugeot 505 automatic, on which he'd had hand controls built, so I could use it when in Kenya and my mother would drive it when we were in England. We didn't own a car in England. My mother-in-law had, incredibly kindly, given us the use of her lovely black Daimler with red leather upholstery. I couldn't drive it, of course, it had no hand controls. Our farm had been confiscated by the government. The circumstances of which I'll tell you about later. For our part of the investment given to my father, would just cover the cost of a personally built Mercedes 300 D with hand controls. So there it was, all set up, an amazing piece of good fortune, arising out of the worst of circumstances. Since the accident, I've come to realise, not soon enough, it's most important to try to find something positive, out of any misfortune. If you can't, it'll weigh you down, and crush you out of existence.

All we had to do now was get ourselves to the Stuttgart factory at the appointed time and date. Easy you may think, but no, nothing is ever easy when newly paraplegic, and nothing would have been achievable without the efforts and determination of my ever stalwart and ingenious Little wife.

By the time we received the call to say the car would be ready for collection, we were back in London living with our wonderful fairy godmother, Marriott. By chance, my wife's younger brother Alexander was off skiing in his camper-van. He suggested, with a small deviation, he could drop us off on the way. Wonderful. Setting off to Stuttgart, to collect a new Mercedes Car, was almost as exciting and daunting as setting off to India to find an unknown Guru to tell me all my ills would be over. For a newly injured paraplegic, confined to the limitations of a wheelchair, to be given the power and freedom of a modern motor car, is as to be given wings.

We'd found a somewhat inexpensive hotel in the centre of the city that catered to our needs. It was from there we sallied forth exploring for a couple of days prior to the collection of the vehicle. That evening, while pushing about the central square, we came upon a very friendly, welcoming little restaurant, whose light white, cold Riesling house wine was irresistibly inviting. I'm coming up to the central component of this little tale, that always brings you down-to-earth, whenever you think you might have got the hang of things. The house wine there had a very low percentage alcohol, so polishing off a litre carafe around delicious food, served with such grace and warmth, was quickly replaced, by another carafe. All too soon we'd come to the end of our lovely evening, so I called for the bill. While taking out the money from my bumbag, I glanced down at the very pretty tiled floor. Oddly, underneath the table and all around us, was a great pool of clear, pale yellow water with a strangely reminiscent odour. I said to my wife, 'I wonder where on earth all this water...' I didn't finish the question, we just looked at each other and froze. Simultaneously, we knew. Oh God! I slammed down a wad of money, and we fled. We didn't stop fleeing for five minutes. Crashing up and down curbs, racing across streets without looking either way, until we were both sagging from lack of breath. If they'd cared to follow, we wouldn't have been hard to find. A trail of slightly pungent liquid which was now beginning to form another pool led directly to the open tap of the bag on my left leg. I hope to goodness, the wad of money slammed on the table, adequately compensated for the awfulness I'd left behind, and I can now only apologise profusely.

A taxi deposited us at the collection point. It wasn't long before a deep, dense brown, bright new, gleaming, Mercedes 300 D, purred into view and stopped directly in front of us. Suddenly, there it was, majestically awaiting its owners. The driver, with an air of bored nonchalance quickly showed us about the car, as though it were something people did every day. He was right, of course, not only did people do it every day, as far as he was concerned, they did it every hour of every day. As he threw us the keys while walking away, he said over his shoulder, 'And read the manual before you leave.' Read the manual before you leave, it takes two years to read a manual.

We were alone with our beautiful new car. I slowly wheeled around it just looking at it. Odd, when you come to think of it, an inanimate lump of metal, but for most of us, buying a new car, is one of the major investments of our lifetime. We opened our doors with the softest, almost soundless of pulls, and slowly climbed in. The indescribable smell of new leather upholstery is, well, indescribable, it's like no other, it is simply 'plush'. It wasn't for another forty years, when our Dear Uncle Peter, five years before he died, said, 'I'd like you to have the pleasure of smelling the interior of a brand-new car again,' So he bought us a sparkling new VW Passat estate with beige leather upholstery and a walnut dashboard. We sat together in the new car, inhaled, then laughed out loud. There wasn't any point in explaining the joke to the mystified salesman. An expensive joke!

Sitting behind the wheel of this glorious new car produced the same reaction as it did, all those years later with Uncle Peter in the sparkling Passat. We looked at each other and laughed out loud. The pleasure of driving in this faultlessly designed machine, lasted for seventeen, totally trouble free years, covering more than two hundred and fifty thousand miles.

One of the many banes of a paraplegic's life is how to prevent a pressure sore forming, on your bum, from sitting too long in one position. We'd been taught to raise ourselves, by pushing down on the chair's arm-pads, once every ten minutes, and to stay raised for ten seconds. That's all very well in theory, but in practice, it's not really feasible.

In those days, cushions weren't designed as they are today. Then, what was thought to be the best, was thick sheepskin over a softish piece of foam. Sounds ideal, so that's what I had. However, if you don't do your lifting, you'll more than likely get a red patch at the end of the sacral bone, in the middle of each skeletal bum cheek. If a red patch isn't immediately acted upon, by not sitting on it, it could take up to six months of lying on your stomach for it to heal.

By the end of the first day, even though we'd frequently stopped for a ten-second lift, I had a dangerous red patch at the end of the sacral bone on my right bum cheek. If it didn't soften from angry red to a pale pink, within an hour, you have a problem.

'Ground control, we have a problem.' It still hadn't gone by the morning. Fortunately, my little wife had her driving licence with her, foreseeing such a problem. She took over the driving for the second day while I lay flat, with the back of the passenger seat down, my body rolled to the left to take all pressure off that dangerous red patch. She wasn't used to driving on the wrong side of the road in the right side of the car! So we made slow progress. She did however, enjoy the power and lightness of this beautifully designed machine as much as I did. She drove it frequently when we lived in the East End of London in our extraordinary Warehouse on the River, and there after.

It didn't matter in the slightest making such slow progress, we might as well have taken forever. Our second night stop was memorable for all the wrong reasons. The little hotel had a ground floor room in a very pretty little village, I don't remember where, on the edge of a wandering stream. The menu sounded delicious and a carafe of red wine would go down a treat. The red patch had thankfully started to fade so I'd probably be free to drive the following morning.

Before supper we both thought it would be very luxurious to have a lovely hot bath in the deep, roll topped bath invitingly awaiting. Generally, we shared the same water, my wife would get in first because she liked it very hot, then I'd get in after her when the water had cooled sufficiently for me. A habit left over from my childhood in the Kedong Valley, due to the scarcity of hot water. Tonight though, I said, 'I'll get in first, you can top it up with hot water if you need to.' One of the many things I was taught by my pretty blonde physiotherapist Sally, at Stoke Mandeville hospital, was to be able to get in and out of almost any bath. The most difficult is a sunken bath. How on earth do you get, from the bottom of a sunken bath, a foot below ground level, back into your chair? I can't tell you but I still, after forty years in a wheelchair, manage, if necessary, due entirely to Sally's teaching.

I ran the hot water and took off my clothes. That's not as easy as it sounds. To take off your clothes while sitting in them, and only moving your legs by picking them up, was again, taught to me by Sally. But it does take longer than just, 'taking off your clothes.' I returned to the bath naked. It was more than half full. I cannot think why, but I didn't test the water before starting to get in. I faced the bath, on the side, about halfway down, with the taps on the right. I picked up my left leg and placed the foot into the water. I couldn't feel anything, but I noticed it suddenly turned a peculiar colour and the skin was bubbling. I put my hand in the water. Oh God, it was scalding, it might as well have been boiling. Even my fingers, in that mini second, were burnt. I hauled my foot out, but it was too late. The whole foot was a bubbling, sulphurous mass of half cooked meat. I almost fainted at the sight if it. I nearly fell out of the chair, saving myself in the nick of time. My wife immediately knew something was wrong. She came running naked into the bathroom. She took one look at my foot, and sank to her knees with a gasp of horror, holding her face in her hands, 'Oh no, Oh no, we must put it under the cold tap.' That was easier said than done. I had to manoeuvre the chair to be nearer the taps. I had put my legs down on to the footplates before I could move the chair. It was impossible to lower the level of the water, the plug didn't have a chain. I finally reached the cold water tap and ran the water over the foot. There was nothing else to do. My wife couldn't say anything. Her face was drained of colour. She dressed as quickly as she could, and flew from the room. At the front desk, they realised there was an emergency and she needed a doctor. Quite soon, considering, the doctor arrived on a Vesper scooter. He took one look at my foot, "Oh Mon Dieu," His first reaction was that I could feel it, and put his hand on my forehead to comfort me. He knew exactly what to do for the foot. He hurriedly wrote a prescription and somehow explained it was for a cream that must be applied every two hours for the next two days. The chemist was closed, but he rang them and explained the dire necessity. The chemist wasn't in walking distance. My poor little wife had to drive our brand-new beast, into an unknown village, in the dark, find the chemist, who expected her, get the cream and find her way back to the hotel.

I'd completely ruined what would have been a lovely evening, bringing to an end a very successful little trip. Now we slunk back, our tails dragging on the floor, to our burrow in the Mews, to be comforted by our wonderful Marriott. On hearing the dreadful tale she immediately opened a bottle of champagne. She always kept on ice, 'Forget all that, darlings, forget all that, here's to the new freedom your beautiful new car will bring.' We finished the bottle then she rustled up a delightful supper washed down with a couple of bottles of red wine. What an amazing person. I don't know what we would have done without her.

Prep School

If I could divide my life into chapters, the first chapter would be from the time I could first remember until I was nine. At nine I was sent away to a boarding preparatory school, about a hundred miles away from the beauty and perfection of the Kedong Valley. I didn't appreciate the actual beauty at that age, but I know my sister and I felt it deeply. Occasionally we were taken to children's parties and I distinctly remember wondering why the parents of my 'friends' had chosen to live in the manner they were. Their houses were right next to other houses, the houses themselves were alright, but why so small. And the garden was so small there was nowhere you could possibly hide or build structures. Usually, there was only one tree, can you imagine, just one tree? Nothing to climb, no natural swimming pool, there was no warm water silently rising through little holes at the bottom of the pool. And where did the cook get his fresh fish?

So when I arrived at this preparatory school, after an endless train journey and hours in rickety old lorries on terrible roads. I stood in the middle of a long room, crammed with beds on both sides and I thought, if my Mummy and Daddy, who I loved more than anything in the world, other than my ayah of course, and I knew loved me, could see where they'd sent me, they'd realise they'd made an awful mistake.

It wasn't a mistake and this sort of thing went on and on and on both there and in England until I was seventeen. One day very close to the end of a wonderful holiday, we were in my Aunt's extraordinarily beautiful house overlooking the whole creek where the big ships came in to unload their cargo in Mombasa harbour. I said to my mother, rhetorically really, 'do I *have* to go back to school?' She said 'of course, not Darling, not if you don't want to.' I couldn't believe what I'd just heard. I held my breath. 'I'll ring the Headmaster as soon as we get upcountry.' I thought, I wonder if I'd asked this earlier, would I have got the same response? Have I endured nine years of absolute hell just for the lack of asking!

***

That was the second chapter. The first chapter is really quite brief because it was so idyllic. We lived in this extraordinarily beautiful place. It was like living in the Garden of Eden. My brother sold it to a wealthy Indian family who do seem to realise what a gem they've acquired. It is an oasis, with dry dusty scrub all around. From this parched landscape you burst upon a luscious water world, with huge wild fig trees, long elegant boughs sweeping down to touch the water with a kiss. A long natural pool, maybe a hundred yards long by about twenty-five wide, where the water is crystal clear and the whole pool is teeming with tilapia and freshwater bass. Above and below the long main pool there are other smaller pools with the water tumbling out over the rocks between them. A profusion of massive water ferns and exotic native water flowers throw out a rainbow of misty colour through the dappled light allowed to twinkle by the foliage of the majestic wild fig trees high above.

All around this staggering setting there are huge open, bright green lawns with high terraces set into the hillside so the lawns could be flat. At the bottom of each terrace, of which the support walls are made of lava rocks found all around in the scrub, there are deep flower beds filled to overflowing with the most colourful exotic and cultivated flowers and foliage. People seeing it for the first time just stand and gape, wordless. Stone steps are cut into each terrace taking you to the top plinth where the house is built, also made from hand-cut grey lava. The view from the house veranda looks out over the magnificent garden and river and on to the floor of the great Rift Valley, teeming with plains game. In the distance, proudly standing nine and a half thousand feet high, is the volcanic Mount Longanot. Extinct but still producing enough steam to turn turbines that will keep Nairobi going with all the electricity it needs, well into the future. But I digress, back to the garden. A ribbon of fig trees that follows the river down on to the valley floor is a pathway for troop after troop of monkeys and baboons. The most delightful are the Columbus. Their long, floating black-and-white designer gear makes them look as though they're leaping from branch to branch in slow motion. The Vervets, the Sykes and Baboons, squabble a bit, but only out of 'attitude', nothing serious. There was ample for all to go round; until the end of the season when our orchards would be raided! Then, of course, there was the array of birds, water birds immediately on and around the long pool. The Kingfishers, spotted, with its distinctive cry, and the small one, making a flash of blue and red as it dives in, to immediately emerge with a silver tiddler wriggling in its beak. The Cormorants, usually standing on a low bough hanging low over the water, their wings outstretched, drying before taking their next plunge, often emerged the other end with a fully grown Tilapia in their bills. You'd never think it could possibly fit down that slender neck. Our little pack of five dogs were fascinated by the cormorant's antics. So when it was on one bough or the other, at either end, they'd all plunge in and swim, as fast as they could, to try to catch it. The cormorant would quietly dive in, swim underneath them and come up the other end. They'd swim about in confused circles, bumping into each other, dipping their heads in the water trying to look for it. Then one of them would spot it the other end, already with its wings stretched out and they'd charge off again when exactly the same thing would happen. This game would go on and on until the dogs were utterly exhausted. With their last ounce of energy they'd swim ashore and wearily haul themselves out, long tongues hanging, panting, heads down and flop on the grass around us. While all this life was going on, near and on the water, the deep beds of flowers attracted countless hummingbirds. Their bodies motionless mid-air, their wings beating in a blur, their long curved bills dipped deep into the flowers, to drink the delicious nectar. The soft hum of the bees busily collecting the pollen to make the honey we had every morning on the hot bread made every day by the cook, Churchy. The Bee-Eaters all sitting close together on the telephone line; somebody counted ninety-one varieties of birds in and around the garden. My Sister and I lived and played in this paradise, looked after during the day by our beloved Ayah, Adijah, (Di-Di), and by night our beloved parents, all this magical beauty for the first nine years of our lives.

Why did it have to end, why was it I found myself in the middle of this awful dormitory, with bed after bed packed down each side. 'Come on, come on,' shouted a fat woman in a green dress, 'choose a bed and don't forget which one it is.' She turned on her heel and slammed the door. I think that must have been the moment I put my mind in neutral and did what I was told, for four wasted years.

Well, to be fair, it wasn't entirely wasted as far as I, personally, was concerned. The family who owned the school, had a stable of beautiful horses, so riding was part of the curriculum. If you had experience, which I did as we rode a lot at home all over the farm in amongst the herds of game, you'd be given a horse of your own, and a syce (groom).

My horse was called Thistle, he was a gelding, shining pitch-black, his neck was too long and low to make him a beautiful horse, but we took to each other straight away. He had a fluid trot and a long, languid canter, and when he galloped you felt you were flying. I loved him. Although he had bit and curb, I never had to touch the rains or pull him up, he had the softest mouth I've ever known. I asked Mrs. Foster, the owner of everything, even the Headmaster, who didn't count for much as he didn't ride, if I could at least take away the chain. She wished I could, but it was safety rules. 'Health and safety,' even then.

She was an incredible woman. I never saw her out of her jodhpurs, whatever the time of day. Hers was the beautiful Grey, an Arab Stallion. They were as one when she was in the saddle. No one else ever rode him. On one occasion when on a ride with her, we had to follow her in single file.There were about eight of us, along the side of the main road, an appalling, dusty road, but the main road to Eldoret. Suddenly a bus appeared behind us driving far too fast. She waved to the driver to slow down, but he took no notice. We were engulfed in a thick cloud of dust and the horses pranced all over the place, it was lucky no one fell off. She was furious, instantly in a rage, she and her stallion turned on the bus. I'd never seen a horse move so fast. They caught the bus up; she started to whip the side of the bus, she reached the driver's window, it was open, she whipped the driver himself, yelling at him to stop. Amazingly he did. She ordered him out, he got out, he stood in front of her and her stallion, who was now breathing very heavily, wide nostrils, sitting back, pounding his front hooves. The driver was cowed by this force he was facing, he just looked at her astounded, mouth hanging open, then weakly said 'I'm sorry Madam.' She was now in control of her rage, she said forcefully, 'always slow down when you pass children on horses.' I'd temporarily forgotten I was a child. She never treated anyone who could handle a horse, as a child, you simply understood horses, as she did and that was that. The driver said, 'Yes Madam, I'm sorry Madam.' He climbed back into his bus and slowly drove away.

At the end of one term my mother and father came to collect me. I was usually put on the train and was met at Longanot station. But this term my father had some business in Eldoret. I was so excited I forgot to say goodbye to Thistle and Mrs. Foster. The holidays were so full of doing such exciting things; driving about the ranch with my father, going out at night in an open-top Land Rover with a spotlight to shoot Thompson's gazelle. There was riding, playing about in the garden with my sister, swimming and fooling about in the pool for hour upon hour. The idea of school was way away in the back of my mind. Then quite suddenly, that dreaded time that dreaded train was the day after tomorrow, that awful hollow feeling in the pit of your stomach, all enjoyment gone.

The only thing I could latch on to was riding with Thistle. As soon as there was a gap from unpacking the trunk and pushing the tuck box under the bed, fighting, showing off feats of strength; which all boys seem to have to do while growing up. Then we dashed up to the stables to greet our horses. Thistle wasn't in his usual box. I heard Mrs. Foster coming into the yard. I ran up to her to say hello. I was surprised how pleased I was to see her. I said, 'Where's Thistle, he's not in his box?' Quite suddenly her eyes filled with water, overflowing, dribbling down her cheeks and falling on to her shirt, I didn't know what to do, what to say. I didn't know 'grown-ups' actually cried, especially Mrs. Foster. She said, 'He had to go to the army.' He had to go to the army? What on earth was she talking about, 'He and a few of the other horses had to take the soldiers into the forest,' she hesitated interminably, 'and Thistle was killed.' I stood and stared, jaw hanging, Thistle was killed, Thistle was killed, why was he killed, how was he killed. We just stood and stared at each other, I couldn't hug her, she couldn't hug me, tears were still pouring down her face.

She pulled herself together, embarrassed, 'Let me introduce you to someone else.' I followed her numbly to another stable. Inside was a little black horse with flecks of grey shining through her dense blackness. She was very pretty with a long black mane, a short, curved, high neck, but nervous and wide-eyed. She stood at the back of the stable not looking out over the yard as the others did. Her name was Mazy, she wasn't a horse she was a pony. Mrs. Foster said, 'I'd like you to calm her down, she's too nervy for the small children, stay with her, see how you get on.' She turned and left us together. It was too soon really after hearing of Thistle's death, perhaps she sensed a reticence but we got on quite well. She let me softly stroke her neck, hold her head, blow on her lovely soft nose; I stayed with her, talking to her, telling her I'd be riding her from now on. Her eyes stopped staring. She seemed to relax a bit. I left her box, walked sadly across the yard to go back to the school. I looked round; she was at the front of her box with her neck in the V of the stable door, taking an interest. Perhaps we would get on.

The whole school was surrounded by a tall Cypress hedge, grown in a large square, enclosing about five or six acres. It seemed then as though it were about twenty feet high, but as we were all so small, it might well have been half that height. Whatever the height, it served various important functions. The whole area was on a slight slope with the school buildings more or less in the middle. The boy's dormitories, the sanatorium and the dining room, were at the top of the square and the girl's dormitories on the left looking down. I'm being precise for a very good reason, so please bear with me. At the bottom of the square, in the middle of the hedge, there was a small U-shaped gap, about five foot high and about two foot wide. And it was through this hole, all the boys, during daylight hours, turned left, to empty their bowels while sitting on a plank. This had some holes cut in it, over a deep hole dug down through the red earth, about fifteen feet or so. Turning right through the hedge they'd empty their bladders directly into the African bush. The girls were wimps, so they were allowed back into their own house for their ablutions during the day.

So the perimeter hedge was a useful tool to keep us all in, and the rest of Africa out. But a crucial factor as far as us boys were concerned, we could disappear, into the hedge, melt away. A signal given by a chosen spotter for the day, whenever a teacher unexpectedly appeared, a full playground of children would melt away, with no sign of being there at all. Another thing we could do was climb up through the hedge and pop out at the top of the hedge. It must have been quite comical to see a line of small boys, sitting, arms folded looking out at the scene all around. One day, on the outside of the right of the square, quite a big bush fire had started in the parched dry scrub beyond the hedge. A group of us, the riders, the top dogs, climbed up through the hedge, popping up at the top, to see how close it was getting. We were completely unaware of the danger in which we were putting ourselves. One spark would have sent the hedge up like a tinderbox, that was the reason all the farm workers were gathered doing their utmost to beat it out.

Mrs Foster had a daughter. Oh my goodness me, did Mrs Foster have a daughter. She wasn't an ordinary girl like our sisters or all these girls in the school, she had come from somewhere else, she was from another planet. She was eighteen and she'd just left her secondary school. She was tall and slender with short blonde cropped wavy hair; she could ride, she could play polo and she could run. She ran properly, like an athlete, not prissy, pussyfooting, with bent arms at the elbows and limp wrists.

After lunch, the whole school would retire to their dormitories, and lie on our beds, completely quiet, for an hour's rest. We'd lie flat out on top of the blanket, arms folded across our chests, and quietly talk about Mrs Foster's daughter. Not in any lascivious way, but how beautiful she was, how different she was, we were so proud she was part of our school. She was our Princess Leia, from

Star Wars, not that we knew anything about Star Wars then. But what she was about to do with the fire, would elevate her from 'Princess' status to 'Angelic' status.

The African workers seemed to be losing the battle against the oncoming flames. It didn't seem to occur to us, perhaps we should climb down out of the hedge, we didn't realise the main reason everyone was fighting the flames was to save the hedge. We just thought, 'Goodness, this is exciting, the fire is getting closer.' Out of the corner of our eyes, we spotted her, running like the wind, she was running so fast her feet weren't touching the ground. She ran towards us, over the burning cinders, and through the advancing wall of flames; she was there, with the African beaters, beating with them. It seemed to us, watching from our perch on top of the hedge, they only started to make progress once she'd got there. Someone said 'She's an angel.' We all agreed, 'Yes, she is, she's an angel.' Once she was there they quickly got control of the flames, or maybe the breeze turned, but in our minds 'she' was the one who'd done it. We slowly clambered down through the hedge to the ground, shaking our heads in wonderment.

The following day, as it happened, she was in charge of our ride for the morning. None of us could speak, we just looked at her in awe. She became infuriated, she said crossly, 'What's the matter with you all, you're normally so chatty.' We couldn't say anything. We just looked at her, coming to terms with our beautiful Princess now being 'Angelic'. It was some time before we could banter with her again. I wonder if she ever knew the high regard in which we held her. I wonder what happened to her and Mrs Foster, and her beautiful stallion. I was at that school for two years, only two years, of my seventy years. And yet, I remember all I've just described, as crisply and clearly as though it were a film played back again. Nowadays, in the present, I can watch a film on television, and a week later have little recollection of ever having seen it. Nothing has the impact it did then. Having said that, there are significant gaps in my memory when all I can remember is unhappiness. What was to come, of course, would be far worse than anything I had ever endured then.

Kidnapped

The rest of schooling, the primary reason I was there, as far as my parents were concerned, was a haze. I always put myself at the back of the class, looked at the teacher so they thought I was listening, and put my mind far away to my beautiful home. I could be driving around the ranch in the open-topped Land Rover among all the cattle and game with my father. In a funny sort of way I quite enjoyed having the time to picture all the wonderful things, I did in the rest of my life. All the teachers, in all my schools, just burbled on, about what, I have no idea. Eventually, however, I was brought back home, and a tutor called Veronica came from England. In one attentive year she taught me everything I needed to know to pass an exam called 'The Common Entrance'. If I'd thought this out properly I should have failed this exam, but I didn't. I passed the bloody thing, which opened the door to another wasted four years in an English school. Yet more tightly packed beds in dormitory after dormitory.

The aeroplane landed at London airport after two days flying from Nairobi. We stopped the night at a little place called Wadi Halfa on the banks of the river Nile in Southern Egypt. It's no longer there, well it might be, but it's been swallowed up by the advent of the gigantic Aswan Dam. I was going to be looked after, when I wasn't at school, by my grandmother, who lived in Tunbridge Wells in Kent. My mother had organised for me to be met by a 'Universal Aunt' to take me across London and put me on a train at Charing Cross, to be met by my grandmother at Tunbridge Wells. I wasn't too keen on the idea of being looked after by my grandmother, I'd met her once before, years ago, and I knew she didn't really like me. The feeling was mutual. So when in Wadi Halfa I bought her an ivory paperknife, carved as a crocodile, to try to placate her. The plan didn't work.

After passing through customs, dragging my vast suitcase, and trolling along the queue of people waiting for other passengers, I spotted a man holding up a card with my name on it. This wasn't the plan, surely a 'Universal Aunt' was a woman. But I went up to him and said, 'Are you waiting for me?' He looked down at me, I was very small, especially standing next to my vast suitcase. He said, 'I've been sent by your Aunt, Mrs. Edwards, to take you back to her house in Hampstead.' This wasn't the plan at all. But I knew I had an Aunt Sheila, and she was Mrs Edwards.

I'd only ever heard of her described as odd. Her husband worked in the merchant navy as a stoker, whatever that was, and one day went to sea and never returned, never heard of again. But it did sort of make sense I was being taken, by this nice chap, to what turned out to be a tiny house in Hampstead. It wasn't a house as far as I was concerned. It had a door, one of a row of doors, which opened on to a tiny bit of grass and then a gate opening on to the pavement. Anyway, she greeted me very warmly and seemed genuinely pleased to see me, which was more than I was expecting from my grandmother. She made me a cup of tea and we talked about this and that. I noticed she didn't ask after any of the family, particularly her sister, my mother. It was getting latish so she said she'd make us some supper, sausage and beans on toast and a glass of milk. I noticed there was some sort of nervous excitement about her. When we'd finished and the plates taken and washed, she quickly sat down in front of me, leaned forward, her elbows on the table. She said, almost in a whisper, conspiratorially, 'Now, I'll tell you why you're here, it's very exciting.' I didn't say anything, she went on, 'I thought your father was a good man but he's turned out to be as bad as the rest of them,' she paused once more. I said nothing, I'd no idea what she was talking about. 'From now on, I'm taking you over and I've found a wonderful school for you.' I was beginning to be worried, 'I've been to see it and I've told the Headmaster all about you, he's longing to see you.' I still had nothing to say, 'You don't have to go to that awful place your parents are sending you.'

***

On reflection, this was the only sensible thing she said all evening, 'I'll be looking after you completely, so there'll be no need for you to go back to Kenya.' Again she paused, leaned back, long arms, hands still on the table, a look of glee on her face, 'Now, what do you think of that?' I looked at her, I tried to say something, I opened my mouth, but nothing came out. 'I know you must be tired, so why don't you go to bed and think about it, and tell me what you've decided in the morning.' I stood up, I said weakly, 'Thank you for supper.' My legs were so heavy I didn't think I'd make it upstairs.

My little bedroom was the smallest bedroom I'd ever seen in my life. The bed had a bare mattress, with three blankets folded on top of one another at the bottom of the bed, and a bare pillow at the top. I closed the door and just stood, looking at the bed. Quite suddenly, unexpectedly, a lump came to my throat. I started to cry, not just cry, I silently sobbed, tears gushing down my cheeks. I laid the three blankets out on the bed and got underneath the second, fully clothed. I don't remember taking my shoes off. I was still sobbing when a blanket of merciful sleep smothered my terror and the next thing I knew, daylight had broken through my curtainless window. I sat up completely refreshed. I still had my shoes on. I'd never got up in the morning so easily.

I knew exactly what I had to do, in fact, I felt sorry for her. She'd planned everything in a state of madness, poor thing. I said, 'I'm very sorry Sheila but I have to do exactly what my parents want me to do, so there's nothing to discuss.' She said, matter-of-factly, 'Then you'll have to leave right now, and I'll have no more to do with you.' I lifted my incredibly heavy suitcase and staggered out of the front door, and before I'd even got to the gate, she'd slammed it shut. I didn't see her again for another twenty years. I didn't even know in what direction I was going. It was a very ordinary car lined suburban street. Just by chance a taxi came into view, I tentatively put up my arm and he stopped. I said I wanted to go to Tunbridge Wells, but I didn't know what station to go from. I couldn't lift my case into the cab. He laughed, got out and put it in. He started to chat, I didn't know they all do of course, so I followed suit and told him my present plight. He was astounded at my pathetic little tale. He couldn't understand how I ever got into this position to begin with. We pulled up at Charing Cross. He hopped out and carried my case to gate number five, buying my ticket on the way. I fumbled about trying to pay him, but he wouldn't hear of it. He said goodbye and wished me the very best of luck. He chuckled and said, 'I think you're going to need it.' I was a day late arriving, but my grandmother didn't seem to be that surprised. I told her what had happened, she didn't say anything, she just looked terribly sad, I thought she was going to cry. It was never spoken about again. Years later we invited Sheila to our wedding and she came with a strange man in toe, whom she introduced as Mr. Johnson. The story about her and Mr. Johnson is an extraordinary story in itself. I'll have to expand on that as I go along.

***

Fast-forward thirty years or so. The telephone rang, I picked it up and a voice said, 'This is the West Dulwich nursing home, Mrs Edwards has just died, you are named as her next of kin. Please tell us what you'd like done with her body?' In a way, I wasn't surprised! She'd have done this knowing it would catch me unawares. 'And please can you clear her room as quickly as possible.' We rang a local undertaker, they knew the Home well, it supplied regular custom. The following day we went to clear her room. Under her bed was quite enough money to cover her funeral costs. We only managed to muster about six people to the service .Ourselves, my little sister, and one reluctant member of staff from the home. A woman from social services came and an odd-looking man crept in and sat at the very back. This formed the entire congregation. Her two sisters, my mother and my Aunt, were both in their care homes, my Aunt with dementia and my mother with heart disease. I paid the undertakers cash, then and there, We followed them to the crematorium and bade farewell.

We had found, underneath her bed, the keys to her house and it was in this house a very strange story began to unfold. Her house was an ordinary little house, two up two down in quite a pleasant street in Dulwich, South London. The first thing we had to do was to find if there was a will.

We opened the front door and the scene that confronted us was so awful, revolting with the smell of decay, and putrefying mould. If it had been left up to me, which it was really, I would have closed the front door, looked on Google for a few house clearance firms nearby, walked the hundred yards to the High St.and told a couple of house agents to sell it. And that would have been that. My wife said that that was taking the easy way out. We had a responsibility which had been, unwittingly, thrust upon us and we were to deal with it to the best of our ability. So that's what we did. But that insistence cost her, her health for a long time to come. The house was contaminated. But it also yielded a very strange story, and quite a lot of money for both my mother and my Aunt, not that they needed any, they were both beyond caring about anything. Fairly soon, in our delving, we came upon the name of a solicitor. My brother-in-law Douglas quickly found the name of the firm she'd used. They were well-regarded and the original solicitor was still there. He was astonished to hear from me. It turned out, more than twenty years ago, my aunt had drawn up a will but had never completed it. He's become a friend and still deals with our wills. On further delving, in box upon box brought out to me in the front garden, if that's what you can call it, many bank accounts began to appear. Not just one or two but fifteen or sixteen. They all had money in them, they all were savings accounts. My mother had felt guilty, as she was relatively well-off while her sister seemed so poor, she'd made regular payments into Sheila's account for years. It was a savings account and the payments my mother had made were all there, untouched. She'd also had regular payments from social security, so they must have come to the house, seen how she lived and made no further investigation.

Another strange thing she'd done was to write all her letters, private or letters of complaint, in longhand, quite neatly and with a carbon copy. This was whether they were to the council, to the Archbishop of Canterbury or the Prime Minister of the day. The points she was making usually started quite sensibly, well considered and often provoked a reply. Her arguments then very quickly became exaggerated, and fell apart. She was a religious fanatic, a born-again Christian, so she often quoted sections of the bible to prove her point.

A lot of her private letters were to Mr. Johnson. She only ever referred to him in that way, his Christian name never came up and she only ever referred to herself in the third person. So her letters would start something like this, Dear Mr Johnson, Mrs Edwards wonders whether Mr Johnson would like to come to tea next Saturday afternoon. Mrs Edwards' Servant, Agnes, will be present so there would be no impropriety.' Poor Agnes was a simpleton. She'd been looked after by social services and one day was taken along to a church meeting for an afternoon out. Her life then suddenly took a dramatic change for the worse. My Aunt offered to give poor Agnes a loving home and look after her. The offer was taken up immediately. While sitting in the front garden in my wheelchair, being brought all theses boxes of papers, the next door neighbours introduced themselves, wondering what was going to happen to the house. We naturally turned to the subject of Mrs. Edwards and Mr Johnson. On hearing who I was, their manner changed remarkably, shocked and reticent. They became lost for words and started to move away and I quickly realised what was happening. I explained her whole family found her difficult, impossible to deal with, so we were going through her belongings to see if we could find a will prior to placing the house on the market. They offered to make us a cup of tea. It's extraordinary how a cup always has a calming effect. So we all sat together, they in their garden and us in Sheila's garden, with the low hedge between us, and talked about nothing in particular. The weather is always safe. Local politics, the council, bin collection, then slowly back to the strangeness and the peculiar behaviour of their neighbour, Mrs Edwards. They'd lived alongside one another for quite a long time and at first got on reasonably well. He'd help her out with small jobs around the house, although she'd never changed anything from the day she moved in. She'd bought the house about twenty years before, fully furnished, even the pictures hanging on the walls. She then became imperious and started treating him as though he were a lowly paid employee. Another example of her behaviour was when my

Aunt Carmen, her sister, had once asked us, as we happened to be driving through Dulwich, to drop in a little posy of flowers just to say hello. My wife was standing there, on the front doorstep, holding her little posy, waiting for the door to be answered. Sheila suddenly appeared, door flung open wide, she half shouted, 'What are you doing here, clear off.' And slammed the door shut. My little wife came back to the car in shock, holding her posy in front of her, and said, 'I've just been told to clear off.'

They were aware of the arrival of Poor Agnes, who, very quickly became a slave. The whole scene was Dickensian. The brown peeling wallpaper, the piles of boxes against the walls and up the stairs and the smell, the smell was repulsive. My wife tracked it down to a drawer in the bottom of a wardrobe where she found a corpse of a cat and a note lying on top saying 'God will resurrect my beautiful Bengy.' My little sister found another box, with another cat, with the same message. The bank accounts revealed she, Sheila, was receiving an extra allowance for looking after Agnes.

Soon after the appearance of Agnes, Mr Johnson moved in. Mr Johnson was a 'preacher'. They were aware of orders being barked at Poor Agnes, then shrieks of jeering laughter when she didn't know what they were shouting at her to do. To give Agnes her due, she must have had more sense than Sheila reckoned on because one day she escaped and scuttled off to the Town Hall, where she was gibbering on in apparent terror. Somebody must have had the wit to realise this poor woman needed help and she very quickly found her way back to her original carers, who immediately summoned Sheila. She burst in, all care and kindness, 'Agnes dear, dear Agnes we've been so worried about you, thank goodness they've found you.' Agnes shrieked with terror, Sheila shrugged it off, 'Poor Agnes she must be delirious at being lost.' At last they did the right thing for Poor Agnes. She lived out her days in a kind, caring home for people in her situation.

While sitting there in front of the house surrounded by papers and boxes, a young, smartly dressed black man, in a well cut three-piece suit, came up to me. He said, in a real cockney accent, 'Would I be right in thinking you might be interested in selling this house?' I said I would be, but there might be a few problems to overcome first. He said he quite understood but could we discuss if we were in the same ballpark first and then take it from there. In no time at all we'd come to an agreement, so we shook on it, and he said, 'Deep joy.' We swapped addresses and solicitors and he said, 'I can't pay for it all now, but I'll put down fifty grand. I'll sell it before starting the building work and with the buyers deposit pay the remainder.'

It would not be possible to imagine something good coming out of someone as awful as my Aunt Sheila. But it did. No will was ever found and Mr Johnson had gone off to meet his maker, so, ironically, everything she owned went to the two people she hated the most, her two sisters. The sale of the house to 'Deep Joy', worked out to the letter. The social services were paid back all the money Sheila had fraudulently stolen and the people who bought the new house 'Deep Joy' had built, were delighted, over the moon. We went to see them later. We did not tell them about Sheila.

English Channel

Now, back to my first boarding school in England. While at this ridiculously expensive school where the classes were purposefully small, so each pupil could have the greatest chance of learning, at least something. I, as explained earlier, had perfected the art of not listening, so learnt nothing. But I did make a very good friend. His name was Christopher Whittaker. Chris was an incredibly talented young man, something I lacked in abundance. He couldn't remember when he couldn't play the piano. He could play anything, classical or show tunes. He could sing the lyrics of shows having heard them only once. He wrote his own, caustic lyrics about all the tutors and performed them in front of the whole school at the end of term. He was a star in the classroom, all his A levels he passed with graceful ease. He could have gone to any University he chose. He chose the University of California to study geology. But his passion, his deep abiding passion, was the sea; Aqualung diving, and the sea. His hero was Jacque Cousteau and the whole purpose of his education was designed around being accepted as part of Jacques Cousteau's team. He wanted to be on his ship Calypso, sailing the oceans of the world studying them in all their aspects, and the effect their changes would have on mankind. Had Chris lived, I have no doubt he would have achieved his aim. He died saving someone else's life. For him, it was doing his duty, but for all of us it was a terrible tragedy.

To this day I have no idea why Chris took me up as a friend but there's no point in wondering, I just have to be grateful he did, because he was responsible for the only two things I achieved at that school, aqualung diving and potholing. More of that later. It may seem odd, but those two activities go together. He made me keep a log of all the dives I did. My first dive was in the freezing cold, muddy, smelly, six-foot deep pond, at the bottom of the field our schoolhouse looked out on. I still have that logbook, it could well have been the only exercise book, I ever wrote in, during the four years I was at that school. He had all the equipment, the tanks, the pressure valves, the wetsuit. Actually, the wetsuit didn't fit me as I was so small. So he bought enough double-sided rubber foam and a pattern and told me to build it myself. As it happens, practically the only talent I have or had is, I'm quite dextrous. So I set my mind to it. In a few days, I not only surprised myself but everyone in my dormitory. I made it on my bed, and the result astonished Chris. Unfortunately, depending on the way you look at it, that wetsuit only lasted me one term, because quite suddenly, my voice broke and I started to grow, I grew five inches in one year. I was in a lot of pain all the time. I kept on going to the sanatorium and saying, 'I ache all over,' it was as though I'd strained my muscles and joints. 'You've done too much training, go away.' You would have thought they could have told me, it must happen a lot at a boarding school, suddenly bursting out all over at that age, it was growing pains.

An attractive blonde American woman called Jane Baldasare, made an announcement in the Daily Mail, she and her husband were coming to England for her to attempt to be the first person to swim the English Channel underwater. When Chris first found the article about Jane and her other record-breaking achievements, he was so excited he could hardly contain himself. There was no question in his mind, 'he' was going to be part of her team on that swim.

The then famous Billy Butlin, of Butlin's holiday camps, had agreed to be her sponsor. He was a excellent choice with his outgoing, entertaining character and advertising skills. He'd also agreed to put up Jane and her husband Fred, in one of his hotels in Folkestone while setting up the whole, very complicated, 'event'.

Chris somehow engineered a meeting. It was a foregone conclusion, with his determination and genuine knowledge of all it would entail to approach such a swim, he was not only accepted, but paid to be a member of the team. However, what she hadn't bargained for, I was part of Chris's own team. She said 'but he's so small.' He said, 'It doesn't matter how small he is, in fact, the smaller, the better.' She had no choice but to agree.

It took quite a long time to set the whole attempt up, as you can imagine. So when she saw me again some time later, having sprouted like a well-watered plant, she stared at me in disbelief and said, 'but how can you be the same person?'

The English Channel is one of the busiest shipping lanes in the world. Very tough training and teamwork was essential. She had to train for the possibility she might be swimming for thirty hours non-stop. The energy she'd be using, against the cold alone, would be a thousand calories every half-hour. For the attempt to be registered as an underwater feat by the Guinness book of Records, the swimmer could not break surface. It was much more efficient for the swimmer to stay at the same depth all the time, and be given the food to feed herself while on the move. A formula of baby food and chocolate Milo, the highest calorie intake with a volume of water to quench thirst, was mixed and poured into a rugby football bladder and given to her every half-hour.

She did very well and became incredibly strong. Unfortunately, she made two attempts and failed twice. It wasn't her fault in any way. The first failure was caused by a stupid muddle on the boat, and an empty air cylinder was taken down to replace hers. Can you believe it? On the second attempt, Chris was put in charge, but the weather got so bad the divers could no longer get in and out of the boat with the food and air cylinders. It was quite calm down at twenty feet, it was very difficult to persuade her to come up. She was so disheartened she couldn't try again. I don't blame her. Her husband got so fit training her, later he made an attempt himself and did it. It took him over thirty-two hours. So he, Fred Baldasare, was the first person to swim the English Channel underwater. There wasn't much coverage in the press, possibly because he'd left his wife now that she'd decided not to continue a record-breaking career. Or maybe because she'd left him for one of the pressmen aboard from the Daily Mail.

The school I attended was one of the most expensive in England, so most of the boys had a reasonable amount of spending money. I was the exception. So Chris persuaded a boy, called Simon Paterson, to set a record for swimming the English Channel underwater, in the shortest possible time. To do so would be even better than doing it for the first time. So we set about training. And my god did we train. All Simon was allowed to do was eat, sleep, and train. Simon wasn't a big person, but he was very wiry. He got leaner and wirier, stronger and stronger. You could see his strength growing in the bounce of his step and the way he flew upstairs. I rather envied him. But the envy soon waned while watching him being forced to swim faster and faster, up and down that bloody village pool for hour upon hour. He begged Chris to let him get out, 'No, just a few more.' 'You said that an hour ago.' 'Just a few more.' He outgrew the pool, now he had to endure the cold, up and down that awful beach at Folkestone. Chris shouting at him from those pebbles, 'No, you can't get out, faster, faster.' We were working to a deadline. The Channel shipping authorities couldn't allow too many swimmers to attempt a crossing, it's quite dangerous as it is. The time was soon upon us. We'd had a frame of a cage built out of two-inch steel tubing. It was twenty feet long by twenty feet deep and five feet wide. It was kept afloat by two forty-four gallon drums tied to each end. The frame served a number of purposes. He could follow the boat and tell the boat, by means of a bell, to go faster or slower. He knew what depth to keep and one of the team of six divers would also be with him at all times without having to swim to keep up. Finally, and most importantly, he could be observed by a member of the Guinness Book of Records.

We started at Cape Gris Nez on the French coast, at midnight, the moment the tide turned to run away from the shore. As the bottom of the frame was twenty feet down the boat obviously had to be quite far offshore. The rules stated the swimmer had to be beneath the surface as soon as it was deep enough to be so, only a couple of feet. So he had to be lead with a cord pulled by a swimmer on the surface. That swimmer had to be very strong to stay ahead of Simon at the peak of his fitness and the impatience of starting. We set a cracking pace. We feared it might be too fast. After six or seven hours, you would have thought he might slow down a bit. On one of my shifts, I could only just make it back to the boat, he was swimming so fast. We were also lucky in having a superb Captain of our little fishing boat. He knew, like the back of his hand, the complexity and position of all the different currents that flow back and forth across that twenty-two miles of water. He would turn the boat slightly into each current, therefore keeping us in as straight a line as possible, without slowing Simon down by turning the boat too directly into the current. He was doing so well we arrived off Dover beach too early. He was swimming towards the beach as fast as the tide was coming out. He asked, on the slate tied to the frame, where he was. We wrote, just a couple of miles off Dover. An hour later he asked again, we told him what was happening, he began to flag. Chris had a little pep-up speech prepared, 'New record, it'll never be broken, poor old Fred,' along those lines. His spirits lifted enough to hang on. We came to the point where the boat could only pull the cage so far, he had to be lead to shore the same way he had to be lead to the cage. I was given that job. It was extraordinary how much strength Simon still had. With all my strength, I was only just strong enough to keep the cord taught. When I walked out of the water first, all the awaiting cameras started to flash me. It was all I could do to stop myself from helping Simon by pulling the cord as hard as I could. He had to make it himself to above the high tidemark. He couldn't stand. He crawled. He crawled so slowly, it was agony to watch. He told me later, he felt as though a ton of lead had been loaded on his back. I think that was the only detail, of all the dedication to gruelling training by Simon and Chris and everyone on the boat, to culminate in this incredible feat, Chris hadn't considered. Simon reached the high tidemark on the Dover Beach, from the high tidemark on the shore of Cap Gris Nez in France, in thirteen hours and forty-seven minutes. I think it's a record set in stone.

The Tutor

Looking back on my life, from where I am at this moment, sitting on a luxurious balcony, in a five-star hotel, looking out through countless coconut palms to the Indian Ocean, with white foam waves crashing on to a golden beach in Kerala, Southern India. At the age of seventy, it's very difficult to analyse how events have come about to enable this to happen.

I've explained earlier how I was suddenly released from having to return to my so-called 'educational establishment', with such ease, with a throw-away line to my mother. I was left dumbfounded. The sense of elation didn't hit me till much later. I can remember that feeling of excitement welling up from the pit of my stomach and bursting into my solar plexus, to this very day. It doesn't happen very often and, unfortunately, is quickly dulled by the reality of oncoming events. What I really wanted most of all was to stay at home, live at home, work at home, work with my father, work on the ranch. If only I could have vocalised that wish then. I didn't, I let events take control of me, rather than the other way round. Chances present themselves, to most people, regularly, but it's only the entrepreneurial spirit that recognises them. I let myself be swept along by events I no longer wanted to be part of. I couldn't say I didn't need any further education because on paper I plainly did, but I wanted to get on living a life I knew I loved and understood. Instead, I was sent away, again, for further education.

There followed an extraordinarily strange, surreal year of being taught by a man who was so 'different' from anyone I've ever met before or since, I can't really categorise him. There were only four of us who lived with him and his wife, in his home, an old vicarage, for that year, but he took it upon himself to teach us everything. When I say 'everything', I really do mean 'everything'. Not just to pass exams, in all subjects, but even how to dress in different situations. Every evening we 'dressed' for supper and we had to make interesting conversation. We weren't allowed to ask for the pepper or salt, we had to be offered it, and we had to know which wine to drink with which food. He gave the two of us, as we were slightly older than the other two, a glass of wine he and his wife were drinking. He talked about it, in 'wine speak', where it came from, the type of wine it was, everything you should know about wine if you like to drink it. He would test us the following evening. We then had to compare it to the present evening's bottle. After supper, we'd troop through the cold hall, to his library to be given an 'English spelling' test. We then chose a book to read quietly before being sent to bed. We slept and did our schoolwork in the same room. Every morning before getting dressed, however cold it was, only wearing pyjama bottoms, we'd shiver our way downstairs to the hall, through the kitchen, to the scullery. There, next to the door leading to the yard, was an old, even for then, long-handled water pump. This drew, after frantic priming and pumping, freezing cold clear water, from the well below, half filling a square butler's sink. The enormously fat gardener-cum-general-factotum was ordered to watch over us having this agonising, thorough wash. Watching us wail in agony, always made his revolting, swollen, close to bursting belly, wobble with mirth.

You would have thought our Tutor, with the rigid attention to detail he'd taken upon himself to distil education into us, would have liked us, or at least had some regard for us. Actually, I think he half hated us. He would, quite suddenly, fly into ferocious, bellowing tempers at any one of us. His face would swell purple with rage, his wide staring eyes, one of which was glass, looked as though they were about to pop out of his head. He'd bellow, at any one of us, 'go to bed', in the middle of any class; obviously we hadn't had enough sleep to be so stupid. He'd get so angry he'd have to storm from the room.

At the weekends, we weren't allowed to stay in our room and footle about being bored, as most teenagers. We had to do something with a purpose. It could be anything, but there had to be a purpose. The local landowner, had a large area of woodland nearby, with a picture-perfect river wending its way through the middle. It would form smallish pools then continue to squeeze its way through large boulders and rocks and waterfalls to the next pool. We were allowed to fish the pools, and we were allowed to make small fires to grill our fish. Catching fish couldn't be relied upon, so we were given small loaves of bread and cheese, or pieces of steak to cook over our fires, or other titbits his wife had over in the pantry. In the telling, it all sounds rather ideal, but somehow it wasn't. Everything was a test, and we had to pass the test, with his unnamed rules, in exactly the same way as if it were a written exam. So a failure might well provoke a torrent of derision which could work itself into a full-blown explosion of purple-faced fury. His expectations were far beyond everyday reality. He wanted us to be his 'Famous Five', all day, every day, it was very wearying. I now can understand how disappointed he must have been, but he was working with the wrong people, we were there because we'd failed elsewhere.

***

The day we were waiting for, the day we were working towards, the primary reason we were there, finally arrived. The local vicar was booked to invigilate. We were taking Maths, English, History and Geography. Early that morning, before six, he burst into our room, shouting, 'Get up, get up, wake those stupid, inert brains of yours,' then stormed out. No sooner than we were struggling to wake, he burst in again, 'Come on, come on, what do you think you're doing.' he was winding himself up into a shouting fury, 'Don't you know what day this is, get washed, have breakfast, come on, come on.' We were sitting waiting at our table in the middle of the room, ages before the vicar was due to arrive. 'Don't just sit there, do something.' He was so nervous, he couldn't stay still. Maths was first, it wasn't too difficult. The Vicar quietly sat there reading, so unlike our 'tutor'. I don't know what to call him really, 'our keeper', 'our headmaster'. He could be heard pacing about down stairs, around the sitting room, through the hall, into his study, in and out of the library, into the garden, slamming the patio doors, he was a caged tiger. At the end of the allocated time the vicar quietly said, 'Please stop writing', and collected our work. This was the cue for our caged tiger to burst in, grab one of the papers and immediately go through the whole thing question by question. 'Oh no, you didn't, you brainless idiot.' No praise for correct answers, just a grunt, 'About time too.' This whole routine was replicated for every subject. He must have been exhausted, but as I said when I started to relate this episode in my life, he was a very 'different' man.

Anyway, the year, eventually, wound its expensive way to a satisfactory conclusion. With all exams passed, maybe not with flying colours, but acceptable enough to allow me back to where I always wanted to be in the first place, In my beautiful home in the Kedong Valley, on the cattle ranch, working for my father.

I'd started my schooling at the age of six and I'd now finished at the age of nineteen. Thirteen years. Thirteen long, long years. Did I really learn anything of any use for 'this'? This is where my heart was, my being, my soul. I was complete here. Even though I knew this is where I should be, I never expressed it in those terms. I knew my father would have done anything I asked of him, but I never put it to him like that. I also knew he didn't really believe farming was a viable way of life. He wasn't 'a farmer', he was a businessman who farmed. It would never have occurred to him he was building something for the future, something to 'hand on' to his sons. If he could have sold everything for an enormous profit, he would have done so.

London

I found myself back in London, no particular place in London, just 'in London'. I wandered the streets of London. I distinctly remember coming up from the 'underground' at Piccadilly Circus, spat out from a hole in the ground, into a teeming mass of people. A moving crowd, I was part of the whole crowd, but not knowing a single person, I was completely alone. I might as well have been in the middle of the Sahara Desert. I moved about unseen, I could do anything, and yet I could do nothing. I had nothing. Why was I here with nothing? In the middle of this teeming mass of humanity, completely alone. I had a loving family, I had a beautiful home and yet I was here with nothing.

I bought the Evening Standard newspaper. I found a room in Nothing Hill Gate for £2 10 shillings a week. It was a brown room, up four flights of brown stairs, in a brown house, owned by a thin, old, bent stick of a landlady. She had iron grey hair pulled tightly back into a bun and wore the same faded floral apron all the time I was there. At the end of each week I padded down the brown stairs into a half-lit brown basement and knocked at a brown door. I paid my faded, bent, little old stick of a landlady, her rent. I could hardly distinguish her from her surroundings. Her tight sallow, parchment cheeks, slowly pulled back her thin lips into a half smile and she said softly, 'Thank you.'

My grandfather was a very, very wealthy, self-made Australian, who built the first sugar refinery in 'Black Africa'. I never met him, and my father never referred to him in any way. My father's nickname, to his seven brothers and four sisters, was Squib. Although he never so much as raised his voice to us, his close family, I had cause to witness his explosive temper on some occasions. I think his temper had a lot to do with the relationship he had with his father.

Later, my father had asked Lord Lyle, of Tate and Lyle, to give his son a job, in the head offices of Tate and Lyle, in the city of London. The order to employ me had filtered down from on-high to the manager of lump sugar sales. I was welcomed with open arms, the prodigal son. I was given my own desk, £10 a week and an account at Lloyds bank in the city. I had 'made it. Well, perhaps I might have 'made it' had I ever discovered what on earth I was supposed to do at my beautiful desk, with its green leather top, drawers each side, and my own telephone. There were nine other desks in the room, with a row of four busy tapping secretaries at the front. Everyone was so industrious, If they weren't scribbling in huge manuals they were talking earnestly on their telephones, or they were walking about quickly from desk to desk. In and out of the office, speaking into dictaphones, pieces of paper flying from in-tray to out tray, the whole office thrummed. I was a fly on the wall, I can see the whole scene as clearly now as I felt it then. I was part of a machine, in the same way, I was of the crowd at Piccadilly Circus, but a spare-part waiting to be used. All the other cogs were in good working order. Lunchtime thankfully arrived. A delicious lunch was provided in a canteen for all office staff, and the managers of all departments had their own restaurant. I met a chap there who'd been working for Tate and Lyle for more than ten years and was relieved to hear he didn't seem to know what he was doing either. He was perfectly happy with his situation and intended to go on working for the company until he retired in 35 years. Could I actually go on doing this for the next 40 years? The thought was terrifying. I persevered for eighteen months.

A few months before I handed in my gratefully received notice, by a relieved departmental manager, I'd turned desperately to the Evening Standard's classified ads looking for anything that might catch my eye. I'd no idea what I was looking for, but suddenly a little two-liner jumped out of the page. Drama classes. Auditions held at 23 Berwick St. W1. 6pm. I knew Berwick St. was well known for its material shops, but I was yet to find out the nature of the other trade for which it was better known. I climbed the stairs up to another brown door. I knocked. The door swung back and in front of me stood, a short, fat middle-aged woman with a cigarette hanging from the corner of her mouth and wearing a flimsy, frilly see-through nightdress. She said, in a broad cockney accent, 'Wanna short time love?' I didn't then know what 'a short-time' was and said, 'No I've come about the drama classes.' The door slammed shut. I eventually found myself sitting opposite a pretty little, round-faced girl, with white, clear skin and large doe-like brown eyes and long dark straight brown hair. She asked me to do my audition piece. I can't remember what I did, but with my fiver on the table I was accepted.

I didn't know then, but do know now, this little meeting, held in such a different place to anywhere I had ever been or experienced, was to have a profound effect on the direction of my life. Not only did I find a group of open-minded friends, from such diverse backgrounds, I'd broken myself free from the chains to which I had willingly tied myself, those of my own background.

My father didn't want me to have anything to do with farming, but I wondered what he'd think of my present choice.

There were about eight of us altogether. At first we met once a week in the back of the little material shop in Berwick Street. But we found we enjoyed each other's company so much, we booked another room in Holborn to meet more often. The classes were taken by the little white-faced, dark-haired girl called Zoe and a Scottish actor called Jeremy Ure. Quite quickly it became apparent who could act, and who just found it liberating to mix with others of open, friendly diversity.

Surprisingly, very surprisingly, I found myself drawn to the whole notion of the theatre. Not necessarily acting in itself, but the whole thing. I'd stumbled upon something where everyone concerned had the same enthusiasm, a sense of envelopment. Only in retrospect can I equate that sense, as equivalent to belonging to my home. A warmth, satisfaction, a calmness. No one could honestly recommend it as a profession, and I can truthfully say the idea of acting at all, let alone a profession was never even a spark. But all those to whom we were introduced by Jeremy Ure and little doe-eyed Zoe, loved doing what they did.

It wasn't long before I was given my first job. A six-month contract as an ASM, assistant stage manager, in the repertory theatre at Northampton. I received the princely sum of six pounds a week. The room in which I lodged nearby cost thirty shillings a week with use of the kitchen. That left me four pounds ten shillings for everything else. Even then a struggle. I don't know how I managed, but I loved it.

Nairobi

When we first met, I was an actor in the small repertory theatre, called The Donovan Maule in Nairobi. I lived in theatre accommodation and my little wife-to-be shared various houses in Nairobi having been invited out to Kenya to stay with a close school friend. Just imagine if she'd known then, what was going to befall her. Even after I'd come out of that loathsome tunnel, she's still left with a raspberry. Cockney slang, 'raspberry ripple, cripple'.

My contract with the theatre was for a year, and the 'Light of my Life' was about to leave any time soon. What to do, what to do, desperate action was called for. I knew she liked the theatre and all the life around it, but my trump card was the garden. Nobody could resist the call of the garden. Every Saturday night the curtain came down at ten thirty, so we made our way out of Nairobi, about forty miles, to my magical home. The main road out of Nairobi, was tarmac, so that was usually uneventful. The magic started as soon as you turned off the main road on to the earth road, my father built, through the forest, down the side of the Great Rift Valley to the house. In our headlights, we might encounter all manner of beautiful animals. Regularly, little Diker would dart out of the undergrowth, come to a grinding halt dazzled by the headlights, wait, then gingerly take high slow steps until back to the safety of the bush on the other side. Less often, but possible any time, were Buffalo, crashing about, Waterbuck, cleverly turning away from the lights showing off their perky white bottoms, to walk down their own shadow. There were sometimes Giraffe, although what they thought they were doing in the forest away from their home on the plain among the little yellow thorn trees, God only knows. But occasionally, very occasionally, and you'd remember it forever, a leopard would be caught by the lights. On the occasions it happened, they didn't seem to mind. They stood there, head up, neck long, full height, alert, looking about, confident. Then they'd turn away from the car, walk-on nonchalantly in front of the lights, as we followed slowly behind. On one occasion, we followed that beautiful, majestic animal for what seemed like ten minutes. At the end of this two-mile exciting drive, even if we'd seen nothing, we'd nuzzle into the car park under the great fig tree, with its long roots hanging from its great bows. The electric light generator had stopped and the night guard was soundly asleep. My mother always left out a hurricane lantern, making an inviting warm glow over the veranda, and inside, on the dining room table, a delicious little feast. Then 'She' went to her room, and me to mine.

Sunday mornings were always a delight. My father was born into a rugged Australian family whose father owned thousands of acres of sugar in northern Queensland, so a sumptuous breakfast was the most important meal of the day. First, fruit from the garden, mine was always avocado pear with cream and sugar, then a Thompson's gazelle's liver and kidneys, and two fried eggs. Then our own bread and marmalade followed by two large cups of the most delicious coffee you can think of. It's the first thing my father 'got on the go' when he came through to the dining room, in the mornings.

I don't think My father was ever seduced by the garden in the same way I was, he liked to be out on the hot plains with his cattle and the plain's game all around. As indeed did I. I can see now that that's where I should have been, by his side where I always had been, before being sent away to England to be 'educated'.

Now, to be an actor, I mean I ask you. He couldn't really understand how that came to be. My father always came back to the garden, every evening, he knew how beautiful it was, but that was my mother's domain. She could do anything she wanted, and she did. She always had a project on the go. My Ayah, Di-dee, who now had no more children to look after, although she still always told me to wear my hat and proper shoes, so I wouldn't get burnt or get jiggers underneath my toenails which only she knew how to take out, now became head gardener. A position she took to like a duck to water, and held until the day she died.

My wife (not yet!) got a job she loved. She worked for the Voice of Kenya, reading the news and presenting programmes, but the thing she enjoyed most of all was reading 'The Book at Bed Time'. It's remarkable how she reads a story or a newspaper article. She doesn't have to read it through first to get the emphasis right, she just reads it and it's always right.

Our year came to an end, almost as though we'd just taken our first breath. The theatre offered me another year, but I said 'thank you but I need to get back to London to further my career.' How could I not have known, going back at that time, was the wrong thing to do for my career. I needed more of what I was doing, I needed experience. I needed as many years as they'd give me. If I had done that, my life would have been entirely different. In retrospect that was a pivotal point. My wife would not be my wife. She would have gone back to England on her own and I'm pretty certain she would not have come back. Instead, what we did was to seal our fate together forever. We drove back to England in a small Toyota Estate my father had given me. He couldn't possibly recommend it for what we had in mind, he'd only given it to me because it had come to the end of its useful life and he was chucking it out.

Another thing, apart from the garden, with which I seduced my poor little, unknowing wife-to-be, was my Aunt Ginger's astounding house on the coast near Mombasa. My Aunt Ginger was a wonderful, unique, eccentric, enveloping individual. Her real name was Penelope, but her hair was bright ginger, and as she got older there was no hint of grey, the ginger simply got softer. But her loving, warm, embracing personality never faded. She died a few days short of her hundredth birthday. Such a shame, she would have loved to have had a telegram from the Queen.

The cruelty of old age had taken her sight and her ability to walk. She'd taken to her bed for the last few years of her life and she held regular audiences for the many, many people who wanted to be with her, laugh with her. She never lost her lovely laugh, she'd close her eyes, her head would go back and a deep chuckle would pour out of this incredible, unique person.

Whatever story you told her, she always said it was the funniest story she'd ever heard!

All the houses she ever lived in, she built and designed herself. She never made a drawing the builders could work from. They had no idea how to price or plan the work before they started. The central theme of her houses, rather like her enticing personality, was to let the outside in, the outside to be an integral part of the inside. So how better to achieve that, than to have no walls, or as few walls as possible. The whole structure of the house was there, ceilings, roof and corner supports et cetera, but you could look right through the house to the view beyond. The house became part of the view, you lived within the view, so the structure of the house and the views all around became as one.

I have a cousin who lives in Australia who took it one step further. When we last saw him, I asked him what was the first thing he would do when he got back home after being away for so long? He replied, 'I suppose we'll have to weed the sitting room.'

So the view Ginger brought into her house was the vast magnificence of the modern ocean-going ships and liners that sailed the world's oceans and then berthed at Mombasa harbour.

She built her house atop a two-hundred foot high coral cliff whose base plunged deep down to form the edge of the creek. All the ships slowly slipped by, with a deep throbbing rumble, to get to their berths. Sometimes, if their berths were taken, and they'd have to wait a couple of days, they'd anchor right in front of the house, filling all the windows with their massive presence. As the tide changed, flowing in or out, they would swing slowly round on their anchor chains. The sterns so close you'd think surely one day, the pilots would misjudge the length of the ship and it would come crashing into the sitting room. All this was, of course, tantalising, enticing, to a twenty-one year old English girl still wet behind the ears.

And now the chance to make a trip almost beyond imagining with excitement and change. Quite understandably her mother was in panic mode. Her beautiful daughter, who she'd brought up with such care and attention to every detail, ready to be launched upon the marriage market to a suitable Englishman from a good background, with a sound income, was about to throw her reputation away. All for a worthless, unknown, out-of-work actor from the colonies. As I look back on that time now, I ache with sympathy.

We vaguely worked out the route of our whole trip, with the help of the AA in Nairobi. They were very helpful. The only thing we could be sure of was which countries we had to drive through to get to England. All the middle eastern ones needed visas for ourselves, and a carnet for the car. If it hadn't been for them it would have taken weeks of trailing around Nairobi from embassy to embassy, standing in interminable queues for hours. Often to be told, when you finally get to the top, 'The office is now closed, come back tomorrow.' I don't know about other African countries, but Nairobi is famous for 'how to tackle a queue'. You have to know how to buy your way along. But the way in which you buy your way along is the art. Only Kenyans know how to do it, and only certain Kenyans specialise in certain types of queues. The AA need to get to the top of queues on a daily basis, so it's vital they do it quickly or else a logjam will build up and they'll cease to function.

You might have thought the vehicle we'd use, for what could well turn out to be quite an arduous expedition, would be a reasonably substantial 4x4. Spare wheels bolted around the body, roof rack, sand filters for the engine, heaters for going across the Alps and through Northern Europe at that time of year, a substantial vehicle. But no, it was a very ordinary, everyday, small run-about, Toyota Estate, my father had chucked out because it had come to the end of its useful life. From our meagre earnings, we'd managed to scrape together the tidy sum of sixty pounds each, which was to cover everything from petrol to food to breakdowns, the lot. Even for then, 1965, it was very little. How we thought we'd manage, I don't know, we just wanted to do it, in our bones we had to do it.

The next task to be addressed was the procurement of a chaperone. Its achievement was probably even more vital than anything else, because without it, there was no chance of going anywhere. Funny now, but not funny then. But how to find one? We knew no one who fitted the bill. After a great deal of discussion we eventually decided to post an advert on the screen of one of the big cinemas in Nairobi, "Girl needed to chaperone unmarried couple to drive to England, for as long as it might take". We went to the performance the evening it was shown. A little giggle trickled through the audience. I think they thought it was a spoof. We had one reply. She was a tall blond German girl called Hanalora, Honey. She'd come to Kenya as an au pair to an English family and her contract had come to an end. Like us, she wanted to do something different and exciting before settling back into everyday living in our home countries. She'd managed to scrape together the same amount of money as ourselves, so we started off on equal terms. She couldn't quite understand the chaperoning bit, but as the three of us would be sleeping together in our little 6ft x 5ft tent, the duty of chaperone wouldn't be particularly arduous.

How we ever thought, living in such close proximity, eating and sleeping and washing and everything else, would work for at least four months, I have no idea. But oddly, very oddly, it did work. It worked well enough for us to be on fond, kissing goodbye terms when we said goodbye in Hamburg. You might say, at least you deserve one night together now, no one would know. Well, you'd be wrong. I drove non-stop, other than a couple of hours on the boat, from Hamburg to Central London, to stay with my Uncle and Aunt, more than 24 hours later. I'd meant us to stay with my grandmother in Tunbridge Wells, but she inconveniently died while we were en route.

***

So, back to the beginning. The start of this trip was, for me, and as it happened for my wife-to-be, the beginning of my life again. I've told you about various episodes, and my education, but the whole direction of my life was without purpose, aimless, drifting about, no idea what I might do from day-to-day. The only thing I knew I had to do was get through the emptiness of a day, only to be confronted with another empty day. My poor parents had done their utmost to give me the best start in life they knew how. It had cost them more than they could afford. When all they need have done was, let me stay at home. I had a completeness at home, a satisfaction, a wholeness. Becoming an actor and joining a repertory company had, for the first time since leaving home, sent away from home, given me a sense of belonging. Being part of something and a direction in which I knew I would like to go. So finding this girl and starting out with nothing, really nothing, which I didn't think a hindrance at all, quite the opposite, we would discover a whole new life together. This was July 1966. We got married on 1st December 1967. No one could have known, just nine quick years later, my life would take a devastating, shattering turn with which I had no idea how to deal. Even now in 2015, thirty-nine years after that dreadful day in June 1976, although we've found a reasonable contentedness and we've achieved quite a lot I suppose, given the limitations in the intervening years, I still feel we're not lucky I'm alive.

So, on that July day in 1966, we three were standing on the upper deck of our elegant 8000 ton Dutch cargo ship, whose name escapes me, watching our little Toyota Estate being lifted off the Quay and onto its deck. This really was the beginning of a journey of a lifetime. There were only three or four cabins on the ship, so we were the only passengers. We'd been invited by the Captain to have dinner with him and his officers, that evening. I asked, as we'd be sailing early the following day if I could ask my father aboard, as there'd be nothing he'd enjoy more than having dinner at the Captain's table. The picture of the meal he'd conjured up was quite infectious. We were all getting excited by the same idea. Oh dear, oh dear. The meal could not have been more ordinary. A few slices of a sort of Dutch cold spam and Edam cheese downed with a glass or two of sparkling water. This was a cargo ship after all. My father could only laugh as he walked down the gangway to the quay and wave goodbye. Early the next morning we sailed majestically past my Aunt Ginger's house, everyone there merrily waving us on our way. The only person who wasn't merry in any way whatsoever was my future mother-in-law. She hadn't given up trying to stop us. She managed to get Aunt Ginger's telephone number and begged her to stop us, or at least send her daughter, her precious daughter, back home.

The Middle East - Part One

Mombasa to Jericho

The first section of the trip was from Mombasa to Kuwait, stopping at Muscat and Bahrain and would take about ten days, depending on Company orders on the way. We've been back to all the same places again recently; you wouldn't know they were on the same planet, the changes are so dramatic. Muscat wasn't a city, by any stretch of the imagination. Looking at the photographs we'd taken then; the harbour was a natural harbour protected by a horseshoe shape of high natural rock cliffs. The small trading port, consisted of a few rows of white Arab-style little houses which almost immediately gave way to desert, with a sand track that ran for about a mile to a date-palmed oasis. What's there now reminds me of the first Star Wars movie, when Liam Neeson goes back to his planet, a few hundred thousand light years away from Earth, turns to his young student, Ewan McGregor, and proudly says, 'The whole planet is a city.' Bahrain is the same. Back then, all those years ago, the taxi-driver automatically took us straight from the ship, to an especially designated beach for Europeans and the Sheik. As soon as we sat down on the sand, an Arab in a full-length white gown came running up with a tray of tea, milk and sugar, and fruitcake.

A couple of days after leaving Mombasa the standard of our evening food suddenly took a marked turn for the better. We were invited to the captain's cabin for dinner. Not only did we have quite a sumptuous meal, it was downed with a couple of bottles of delicious rose wine, probably the only alcohol on-board. It quickly became apparent, however, why this delectable change had come about. The Captain's eye was wandering, and his eye was wandering in the direction of our tall blonde chaperone. She played the game very well. I think she'd had quite a lot of practice. Her timing was perfect. The meals got better and better, the rose wine flowed with ever greater quantities before we contentedly disembarked at Kuwait, without him having his wicked way.

Potentially, a big problem awaited us in Kuwait. Well two really. On docking, I asked the first officer when our car would be lifted off. He paused, he said, 'We sometimes have a little problem here, but I think we'll sort it out.' That didn't sound too ominous. He said, 'go into the city and I think we'll have it off by this evening.' Even then, the city was beautifully laid out. Tall, elegant, gleaming, glass and marble buildings, way ahead of their time, to us country hicks anyway. One of the most noticeable features was the number of extravagantly planted-up roundabouts. The rich density of colour and exotic variety of plants took your breath away. At their pinnacle, they nearly all had the tallest, multi-nozzle water fountains I'd ever seen. Where there weren't fountains there'd usually be a little group of gowned and head-scarfed Arabs, sitting cross-legged on the bright green grass, sipping tea. The tea was dispensed from a colourful teapot sitting on a carved wooden tray. It turned out that tea drinking on the roundabouts had become a ritual and a small industry in its own right. The teapots and the glasses and the trays were all very carefully chosen. The values of a tea set could reach staggering sums. Then there was the type of tea, Indian, Malaysian, Chinese, East African, all the very best, but the most popular tea by far, was tea from a distillery in Scotland, whose name escapes me.

We had our own little ceremony, with real tea, in a cafe that spilled out on to the sweltering pavement. The canopy had dry ice flowing over it and falling to the ground, forming a curtain of coldness, so we remained cool while sitting outside on the pavement. Was that cool, or was that cool.

On the way back to the ship, for Honey to play her dangerous game one more night, because the car was still held hostage on-board, I threw my hands to my face, 'Oh God, I've left my briefcase at the cafe. Stop, stop, turn round, turn round, Oh No, Oh God. Everything was in the briefcase, all the money, the passports, the carnets, everything. Without that briefcase we couldn't move, we couldn't stay, we couldn't do anything. The horror of losing the briefcase made me want to vomit. The taxi-driver looked at me pathetically, and with a half whimsical smile said, 'There is no crime in Kuwait, wherever you left it, it will be there.' 'Please don't try to be nice to me now. Please go back as quickly as you can. You can't realise what this means. Oh no! He turned back at the next roundabout, another little group of Arabs peacefully drinking tea in the middle. It took an eternity to get back to the cafe. Suddenly I saw it, its black leather with brass hinges, there, all on its own, exactly where I left it. All the tables and chairs cleared away, people walking around it, the picture I have of seeing it then, is as clear now, as it was at that moment. The relief, the relief was like a wave of warm water sweeping over me, as I lay on the hot sand of a bright white beach, on the edge of the Indian Ocean. I can feel that wave now, exactly as I felt it then. I didn't deserve that piece of luck, I'd been so stupid. The car was bound not to have been offloaded. I'd used up all my luck for some time to come. No, it wasn't there, we climbed the gangway and there it was, sitting waiting mournfully on the deck. I went to see the first officer. He said, 'The harbour master wants to see you, he's in a cabin at the bottom of the ship, we've given him most of the whisky we use for these occasions. I hope you have a head for whisky, he doesn't speak any English, and he has noticed you have two girls with you.' What on earth was going to happen? The cabin was in the middle of the ship and below the waterline. I opened the door; a wave of the stench of stale sweat and whisky on the breath nearly knocked me over. We both opened our arms wide, greeting each other like old friends and laughed. We warmly shook hands, more laughter, holding both hands now, smiling and laughing. He motioned me to sit, 'Whisky, Whisky,' he said. 'Yes Yes,' I said, 'Thank you, thank you,' more laughter. The glasses weren't like the little tea glasses on the roundabouts, they were ordinary water tumblers. The whisky gurgled in. He said something, I said something. We touched glasses and laughed again. He rubbed his four fingers with his thumb. I knew what that meant, I laughed again, throwing my head back, he did the same and filled our glasses. How long this went on, I really don't know, but the bottle, thankfully, was beginning to run out. Suddenly, seemingly for no reason, he stood up and said, 'OK, OK.' I stood up and said, 'Thank you, thank you,' and we both roared with laughter. We touched glasses and threw our heads back. We shook hands very warmly, laughing all the time, and I moved towards the door. We waved each other goodbye and I closed the door. I had to get to the cabin very quickly, I was about to be sick. I just made it in time before the whole contents of my stomach gushed out. I plainly had no head for whisky. That evening Honey was getting a bit worried about another goodbye dinner with the Captain. As luck would have it, the Officers asked us for a goodbye dinner with them. We gratefully accepted. It was a beautiful evening although the wine didn't flow in the quantities it had on the bridge. It was going to be a long time before we tasted wine again. The first officer said, 'I don't know what you did, but we've been told to unload your car first thing tomorrow morning. So if you're there just after sun-up, you can begin your long, long journey.' The next morning, after many genuine thanks and shaking of hands, we drove out of the port as quickly as was seemly.

***

In Kuwait, petrol was free, so we took advantage of the unexpected bonus and filled any container we could lay our hands on, to the brim. Finally we started that long, long drive to its eventual conclusion in London. We turned to each other and laughed, with sheer exuberance.

Our first night, after an entirely uneventful dull, flat desert drive, was Basra. We had no idea where the campsite was. We stopped a couple of young men, there were only men walking about, not a woman to be seen, who happened to speak English, if they knew where the campsite was. He gave us complicated directions, then said, 'There's no need to go to a campsite, why don't you come to my home and meet my family then you can sleep on our roof.' We'd discussed this exact situation while on-board ship and agreed we must never accept such an offer out of the blue, it was obviously far too dangerous. So what did we all say? 'Oh, that's very kind of you, thank you very much,' and he said, 'Follow me, I'm in that car.' We followed, looking at each other in exasperation, half laughing at our stupidity. As it happened, it was his home, it was his family, we were given a lovely simple Arab supper and we chatted away, very easily, about all sorts of things. There was no alcohol so the evening passed, very pleasantly, until quite late. Just imagine the possibility of those Iraqis, driving around England, and the first Englishman they stop speaks fluent Arabic and invites them back to their house for a meal and to stay the night? That night was one of the most memorable nights I've ever had. I'd done a lot of camping all through my youth, so I was used to sleeping outside, but I'd never slept outside at home. To be offered the opportunity to do so in a little house in the suburbs of the city of Basra, in southern Iraq, on the first night of a trip, perhaps taking months, boded very well indeed. The House didn't have electricity and the few street lights were very dim. Lying on our backs, fully dressed, well tucked up in our sleeping bags, looking up into the deep, dense, blackness of the night, sprinkled with so many sparkling, pinprick dots of thousands and thousands of brilliant shining stars, worlds? I felt a profound sense of being a part of everything. Not just an unconnected part, but a piece, a small piece, of the whole canopy. We didn't speak. We were lost in our own imaginations. The longer I looked up before my eyelids slowly pulled closed, I lost the sense of my own weight lying on the concrete. We drifted away into the denseness.

The following morning, after a simple Arab breakfast, he led us to the main road to Baghdad. We waved cheery goodbyes, feeling very guilty we should be suspicious of such generous hospitality. We looked at each other, thankful for our luck and reluctantly agreed, we must be more careful in the future. Nevertheless, for the first night of our long drive to Hamburg and then to London, it was a lovely thing to happen.

***

It took two days to get to Baghdad. The desert there, is dead flat and featureless. On the way we saw one of many sites that were 'without doubt' the garden of Eden. At Ephesus we saw the Sespian Arch which was the largest self-supporting brick arch ever built, in the whole world, at the time. At Babylon, we stood on a mound of earth that was, supposedly, once the Tower of Babel. We didn't think there was any point in questioning anything, we decided to accept the information, and maybe question it later, which is probably true of most things one's told in life.

I couldn't help having huge expectations of both the Tigress and the Euphrates. All the Biblical stories of great mountains of water crashing together couldn't have been more wrong. To give them their due it was the dry season, but nevertheless they were a disappointment.

We pitched our tent for the first time, quite far from the main Basra-Baghdad road, in this flat, flinty, featureless, silent desert. We were completely alone, just the three of us. So different from all we'd experienced since leaving Mombasa. I said, rhetorically really, looking out on this featureless silence, 'I wish we had a bottle of the Captain's rose wine.' 'As it happens,' said Honey, with a little giggle, 'he gave me a bottle with which to remember him, on our long journey. So I think the first night on our own in this empty desert, would be an appropriate place to remember our lovely little trip from Mombasa to Kuwait' She couldn't have been more right I remember the Captain clearly, to this day.

Up early, with a cup of coffee and a bread roll, given to us by our last night's host, we set forth for the Baghdad campsite. Even then, the sprawl of a modern city takes away all the romance and excitement of coming to a place you've always heard about but never imagined being there. A trade route, the Silk Road, camels with their long rolling gait, bringing their precious cargos of beautiful carpets or spices or gossamer soft silk, weighing no more than a feather. But now the reality is traffic laden roads, honking horns, thick air filled with fumes.

The campsite itself was very pleasing. Well laid-out and maintained, in a date palm grove. From there we set off every day to explore Baghdad. My future Little wife loves to explore cities, as long as she's in a comfortable vehicle. Traffic jams are eagerly awaited. There was no shortage of traffic jams. The golden-domed mosques were outstandingly beautiful. Inevitably, we found ourselves quickly ushered to Baghdad's famous Souk. We weren't disappointed. Huge cauldrons of bubbling hot, delicious vegetable stews, simple fried eggs wrapped in a sandwich of the local bread, hot, sweet, thick black coffee, all tasting so wonderful. The all-prevailing aromas, when walking into the Souk, instantly springs to mind and brings back the detail of vibrant colours of shining silks, of gleaming brass and enticing jewels.

We had intended to stay only a few days in Baghdad and contacted the two names we'd been given in Kenya, so we prepared for the next leg through the desert to Jordan and Amman. While chatting to fellow-travellers in the campsite we began to get reports of a compulsory quarantine camp on the border between Iraq and Jordan. The British Embassy confirmed this indeed was the case, but it wasn't likely to last long as the impracticality of running a compulsory five-day stoppage of everyone crossing the border every day wasn't viable. A political spat between the two countries had caused one or the other, or both, to accuse the other of importing cholera across the borders. The advice was not to go unless you had no choice. We were quite comfortable in our well-equipped site so a few extra days would be quite pleasant. The date palms were groaning with a bountiful harvest, so the extra days of enforced stay wouldn't necessarily upset our daily, very tight, budget. The days, however, turned into weeks and our consumption of dates-with-everything was proving to be rather tedious, to say the least. Suddenly, one morning, the embassy announced the borders would return to normal as the camps were growing exponentially. We were given authority to drive, unhindered, into Jordan. As you might expect, this piece of advice turned out not to be entirely accurate. We were allowed to drive out of Iraq, but there lay the ambiguity. Between the two border posts was ten miles of no-mans land and our authority didn't, necessarily, allow us into Jordan, even armed with our visas issued in Nairobi. We, very tentatively, drove through the ten miles of desert, only to be confronted by a sprawling mass of line upon line of tents and lorries. There was no question of us staying here. We turned and drove back to Iraq. We were greeted warmly with lots of smiles, long-lost friends. Can we please go back to Baghdad. 'Of course, of course, can we see your papers.'

'We can't go into Jordan, so can we go back to Baghdad.' 'Yes of course you can go back to Baghdad, but can we see your papers to come into Iraq.' We looked at each other with the realisation we were being 'played', hooked trout on a line. I've never enjoyed fishing since. As we turned to drive back to the Jordanian border, I looked in the mirror to see their heads thrown back with guffaws of laughter. How is it border police are the same the world over?

We, very cautiously, stopped at the Jordanian border to try to bluff our way through. After all, I did have two beautiful women in my charge, and they were the only two females in the whole camp. They might cause quite a commotion. They seemed to genuinely appreciate that my two beauties could, potentially, be a problem. However, there was no question we had to remain here for five days with cholera tests taken each day. The only concession given us was to deem my beauties incapable of carrying something so obnoxious as cholera. They would be excused the daily testing, and we could pitch our tent away from the rest of the camp. The daily testing each morning entailed joining a queue, with everyone in the whole of this ever expanding camp, all male, of course, waiting their turn. At the top of the queue we dropped our trousers, turned around, bum in the air. A short stick with a little piece of cotton wool at the end was shoved up and then returned to its own glass tube. It was sent off to the lab for testing. No cholera was ever found because there was no lab that could possibly handle that number of samples, and test them all, every twenty-four hours.

The desert there was composed of dead flat black shingle and sharp sand. Although our little tent was pitched quite away from the thundering trucks, lines of tents and hundreds of drivers with their retinue, we never seemed far enough away to perform our morning ablutions, unseen. The first morning we walked and walked until we were specks on the horizon, By the fifth day we happily wandered only fifty yards before digging a shallow hole with our trusty little shovel, and squatting over it!

In retrospect, those five days turned out to be a surprisingly interesting and fun experience. Interesting because we attracted a small but continuous trickle, of fellow English travellers, all male of course. We had enough food for the five days, clean drinking and washing water, topped-up from the border post and something that proved to be remarkably popular, a very large tin of Nescafe. All the visitors were completely different characters, but the common theme, which made us all instantly at ease with one another, was travelling with practically no money.

Early the final morning we awoke with butterflies in our stomachs when we presented ourselves to the officials to restart our journey. With broad smiles they said they'd like us to stay longer, but they couldn't make up any more reasons to hold us. With much shaking of hands and a man-hug for me, off we flew along the straight road to Amman, the capital of Jordan. It was a bit of an anticlimax after all we been through to get here, over the last month, we just made a quick tour of the centre of the Old City, the Amphitheatre, and a Mosque. We then sped off south to an eagerly awaited destination of The Rose-Red City of Petra. On the way, there was virtually nothing of any interest to see or do but drive, as fast as we dared, along straight, empty, new tarmac roads to get to Petra, before nightfall, find the campsite and pitch our friendly little home.

However, there was one little amusing incident that unexpectedly sprung out along a particularly dull piece of desert road. We could see a long way ahead, and we noticed, parked on the side of the road we were driving, a long, black limousine type car, with a man in a dark chauffeur's uniform leaning against the front right wheel arch, and a shortish man with short dark hair and a dark moustache, in a pale yellow Airtex type shirt and khaki slacks, holding a cup of tea or coffee. We slowed, wondering if we might be asked to stop and help, but the man in the pale yellow shirt and dark moustache waved and smiled indicating no problem. We happily waved back as we passed saying 'that was nice and friendly,' and drove on without any further thought about the incident. It may have been as much as five minutes later I suddenly put my foot on the break and screeched to a halt. Both girls simultaneously half shouted 'What's the matter, what's the matter', I said almost shouting,'That was the King of Jordan, The King of Jordan, has just waved to us.' 'Don't be ridiculous,' said Honey, but C. (wife to be) said hesitantly, 'Yes, it was I can picture him clearly.' She has an unusual ability to recognise anybody, even from afar, from behind, or the way they move. We all laughed out loud and continued on our way

The small township outside Petra was distinctly unimpressive. A campsite was marked on the map we were given in Nairobi, but there was no sign of it anywhere. We stopped at the Police station to ask if they knew where it was, 'No there's no campsite, you can pitch your tent anywhere you like.' 'So can we put it just outside here near you?' 'Yes of course.' Then, as an afterthought, the officer who seemed to be more senior, said, 'We have no prisoners at the moment, you can use our cells.' We looked at each other, amazed at the offer, 'Can we have a cell each?' 'Yes of course you can.' It was a night to be remembered. In fact, we must have been there two nights.

The following morning we walked down the hill to a little bedraggled group of underfed, sleepy horses. They perked up when we mounted and walked out well. 'No, no they have all the food they want, this is the way they look. European horses are fat and lazy.' The road narrowed through the steep-sided gorge and turned slightly to the left to reveal the now famous first glimpse of the Rose-Red City of Petra. In those days, more than fifty years ago, there were no other tourists about, so the feeling of discovery, the feeling you were coming upon something so different, so huge, yet hidden, was thrilling. How could it remain undiscovered for so long? The excitement was tangible. Once we started to explore, there were no signs anywhere, it really was a city, it went on and on. We were 'discovering'. Nothing was 'built', no stone cut and placed on another, no foundations, everything cut out of standing rock. Primitive, yet fine and complex, and the colour, a soft, pale vibrant, deep red, for which artists would give their eye-teeth. There was no source of water, there had never been a source of water, so how it ever served as a feasible place to live and trade, I have no idea. It was a fun, exciting, fulfilling day. That evening we returned to our salubrious accommodation in the cells of Petra prison and cooked up a delicious supper, with the policeman on duty as our honoured guest. An early rise and a wave goodbye to our jailers, we set forth across the desert to Aqaba.

I don't know how it happened, but it wasn't until fifty years later, while sailing around the world on our wonderful little ship, the Saga Ruby, we discovered we'd missed a most incredible place. About fifteen miles north of Aqaba is a valley, dividing into other valleys of sheer towering rock. Thousands of feet high, brilliantly coloured in all manner of hues of deep reds and pinks, that is Wadi Rum. I can only suppose we missed it because there's no road to it, even now you can only get to it in a 4x4. My brother-in-law Douglas, the one who'd bought the shares for my mother in Stryker, when I was in Nairobi hospital all those years ago, was with us this time. He wasn't feeling very well, so he lay himself out on one of the long, low tables covered with kilims the local Bedouins use for entertaining cruise ship guests. Like a sacrificial offering, he went sound asleep. The waiters didn't know what to do.

The magnificent immensity of these sheer shimmering red cliffs rising thousands of feet straight out of the sand, had become a magnet for climbers. The driver of our hired 4x4 stopped about 100ft.away from the base to show us all the climbers dotted about the cliff face. At first we couldn't see what he meant, the face was so vast. Then slowly hundreds of tiny dots came into focus. The driver told us they would often take two or three days to get to the top, sleeping on the face.

***

On arrival in Aqaba we couldn't find a proper campsite with all washing facilities etc. so we pitched our tent just outside a nice hotel on the beachfront. We made ourselves presentable and marched into the swimming pool. I can't remember if 'owning' a sun-lounger with your towel, was then acceptable, but that's what we did. The pool faced on to a beautiful white, shining, enticing beach. So with claimed sun-loungers, we dashed into the emerald blue, crystal clear water, for our first, and for me the last, swim in the warm, soft water of the Red Sea. C had, and in fact still has, a bell-like, beautiful, pitch-perfect soprano voice. She was a soloist in her choir at school. The situation in which we found ourselves was so perfect, so dreamlike, she started to sing 'Jerusalem'.

No sooner had she come to the end of the first verse, a la-di-da, barking English voice shouted, 'Good heavens, a beautiful English girl, singing 'Jerusalem' in the Red Sea, how incredible.' He was right. He swam towards us rather like a broad tugboat, creating a wave of water ahead of itself, and introduced himself, in a manner in which suggested we'd know who he was. We didn't of course. 'You wouldn't recognise me with my clothes off, but I'm MP for South Herefordshire.' C nearly sank. He was 'her' MP. This was precisely the situation C's parents were terrified would come about. He even said he'd 'give them a call' on his return. Talk about 'rubbing salt into the wound'.

All too soon we had to be on our way, the Iraq cholera quarantine had caused us to be well behind schedule. We were running out of journey time. We'd divided up our funds into the smallest possible amounts per day, then divided 'that' into the whole amount at our disposal. The fact was we were running out of days for the entire trip.

Jerusalem's old town was then in Jordan, and their youth hostel was clean and well run. It was a thrilling, tingling, elevating experience walking about the narrow streets, knowing only the facade of all buildings had changed over the last two thousand years. The Wailing Wall, the Garden of Gethsemane, the Dome of the Rock, the Mount of Olives, the Way of the Cross, Golgotha. History was laid out before us. We three unnoticed observers, watching people casually going about their business, were wearing the wrong clothing. Clothes, the world over, are out of step with history. The clothes we all wear now, from the rain forests of New Guinea to the streets of London or New York, are all the same. It seems to me contradictory when we're still at war with one another. We send men into space, we travel at over 1000 miles an hour. We eat fresh food grown on the other side of the world the following day. Yet millions starve in the very countries the luxury food comes from. And the Middle East is in turmoil.

At least then there was peace, of sorts, allowing we three to wander happily from country to country, taking in all the beautiful, diverse sights and sounds you could never do today. The Six Day war was yet to happen. It was while in Damascus, being shown around the Jewish Quarter, the Old Town, the silver carvers and the street called Straight, we were told by our self-appointed guide, in a hushed, conspiratorial manner, 'Very shortly, maybe in as little as three months time, there will be a war. The war will involve all the Arab Nations against Israel, which will change everything forever.'

I've skipped way ahead. I must go back to our youth hostel in Jerusalem from where we were well placed to drive to places of biblical history. Bethlehem stood out as the place that made a mockery of all the different Christian religions. The streets of shops surrounding all the holy places displaying thousands of trinkets of such irreverent rubbish, that I, even as a non-believer found incredibly distasteful. Nevertheless, C bought herself yet another long embroidered, ankle-length dress, which she still has, at the Holy Manger Store. When walking down the steps to the crypt where Jesus was born, we passed a large packet of soap powder, Daz, forgotten, forlorn, on the bottom step.

The Middle East - Part Two

Damascus to Hamburg

In Jericho, an incident took place that might have been disastrous. We were driving slowly down a street looking for a sign of the walls blown down by the noise of all those trumpets. There must have been some sort of public holiday, both pavements were thick with the milling crowd. Suddenly, a boy, a young boy, eight or ten, appeared, in the running position, head down, almost in mid-air, directly ahead of the bonnet. I slammed on my brakes, a split-second after I hit him. With a sickening thud, he bounced off the bonnet and hit the road rolling away. A shouting crowd immediately surrounded the car. My door was flung open and I was pulled out. I managed to push my way to the front of the car to see the boy. He was held standing, stooped, held up by bearded men. They too started shouting at me. The excitement generated in the crowd was palpable. It was frightening. There was nothing I could do. I gave in to the jostling, pulled this way and that. Quite suddenly two young men appeared, in their late twenties perhaps, very well built, clean-shaven, wearing grey tea-shirts. They extended their arms, gesturing the crowd to quieten. The effect was immediate, electric. They gestured them to be on their way. Murmuring, they dispersed as quickly as they'd gathered. They turned to me, and in fluent English, asked me what had happened. I explained, and one said he'd take us to the police station. He got into the back seat with Honey. The other one stayed with the boy and the two bearded men. We wove our way through Jericho to the station. He told me to follow him and the girls to stay in the car. The front room of the station was packed with people trying to elbow their way to the top of a queue. My heart sank. This would take forever. The young man said, 'Follow me closely.' He turned one shoulder to the fore and cut a clean line to the head of a queue. A few words exchanged and we were gestured to a door at the end of a counter. A senior officer sitting behind a large desk offered us chairs in front of the desk. The young man spoke deferentially in Arabic to the officer and seemed to explain why I was with him. The officer then turned to me and told me in English, to explain in my own words, what exactly had happened. I did so. He listened without interruption and after a while he said, 'You must come tomorrow to the court, the boy and his father will be there, and the Judge will make his judgement.' On the way back to the car, the young man told me exactly where the court was and reiterated the importance of the time I must be there. I, rather meekly, thanked him; imagine what could have happened had he and his friend not intervened at that moment in the crowd, we shook hands and I never saw him again.

Over supper, back at the youth hostel, we were recounting the story to fellow-travellers when one of them immediately asked if they'd taken our passports. On saying no, they all vehemently insisted we must pack up our things, right now, get into the car, not stop until over the border and into Syria. We looked at each other in astonishment. C said, 'But we've done nothing wrong.' 'What's that got to do with it, you hit an Arab boy, he bounced off your bonnet, tomorrow he WILL be bruised, tomorrow he WILL look as though he's been hit by a car, it's not worth the risk. Just imagine what you might have to pay to his family, it'll take months for the insurance to cover it.' I do hate know-alls. But he could be right. We hadn't thought this through. We had to go away and discuss this privately. C was adamant we shouldn't run away from anything, whether we were in the right or in the wrong. I knew, if I'd hit the boy at all, it could only have been my fault. We were looking out for those bloody walls. I could have been looking away at the moment the boy decided to put his head down and sprint to the other side of the road. That picture is as clear in my mind today as it was then. The two girls couldn't be held responsible in any way, but if I was held in custody, what would they do? Had the authorities purposely not taken my passport; were they giving me a clear signal to leave. The young man who'd saved us from the crowd did stress the importance of eleven o'clock; of course if we just left now, we could easily be well away from the Jordanian border and into Syria.

What we didn't know at this point was, we were going to be incarcerated for another five days of cholera quarantine on the Syrian border.

C was still adamant, Honey was in two minds and I didn't know what to do. But ultimately it was my responsibility. A friend had once told me, if you can't make up your mind which option to take, find a common theme, and take it out, and what you're left with is the essence of the options. Usually, it's with money, take away the cost, then the choice becomes clear. So here, if I ran away, even if I were being guided to do so, I'd be breaking the law. I'd have to live with that decision forever.

We were there, promptly, outside the courthouse, at a quarter to eleven. The girls stayed in the car. I met impassive faces. No hint of anything. I gave my passport to the officer on duty as identification. With just the briefest of glances, I was lead to the dock. I was getting a little nervous.

The boy was smartly dressed in a tidy long-sleeved white shirt and long black trousers. He had an enormous swelling on the side of his head just above his right eye. The bearded man sat next to him holding his hand. Behind them, filling all the other benches, was, what seemed to be, his entire family. I felt very alone. Only at that moment did it occur to me perhaps I should be represented by a lawyer. Were my fellow-travellers, at the youth hostel, right after all. You could hear a pin drop. The door behind the judge's chair opened and the judge walked in. We all stood up and bowed. He sat down. We followed suit. He then said something in Arabic. He then turned to me and said in broken English, 'Tell me what happened.' For some reason I thought the explanation, should be very long-winded. So I started with leaving the dock in Kuwait. After a minute or two he tried to hurry me along. 'Yes, yes, but *yesterday*,' he said. I said, 'I'm sorry Your Honour, but, you see, we were staying at the hostel in Jerusalem, and we wanted to see the ancient history of Jericho, so we were driving along...' Suddenly the bearded man jumped to his feet and shouted something at the Judge, then pointed to the boy. The Judge shouted back and the man angrily sat down. 'Continue' he said to me, 'Well, you see Your Honour, we were slowly driving along the street, there were lots of people...' The man jumped up again, shouting at the Judge, pointing at me then at the boy. The Judge shouted back. But instead of sitting down, the entire family, seated on the benches behind him, jumped to their feet as well, shouting and pointing at me. Quite suddenly the Judge had lost control. There was pandemonium. He tried to regain his authority, hitting his gavel on the desk, but they wouldn't sit down. He turned to me, shouted in his broken English, waving his arm at me, 'You, go, go.' I couldn't quite believe what he was saying, I shifted about, looking around, he shouted again, 'Go, go.' A court official came up to me, took my arm firmly and guided me out of the court. 'Go,' he said. I very hurriedly left the pandemonium and went. I ran to the car and jumped in, 'What happened, what happened,' both quickly said in unison, 'I don't know, but we've got to go right now.' We never did see those walls.

The borders, in those days, before the six-day-war, were entirely different from the position they're in today, and so we headed directly north to Syria. I don't remember exactly how long it took, but it can't have been long, as I don't think we stopped a night anywhere until we were in our prison that night. It wasn't really a prison, but we were imprisoned. Exactly the same little smirks on the border police's faces, as the ones who'd guffawed at us on the Iraqi border, immediately warned us of what we'd expect at the Syrian border. We'd deliberately chosen the smallest border crossing we could find, to avoid all the trucks and, possibly, another quarantine. It was way up in the hills above the northern Jordanian border. No one at the Embassy in Jerusalem had seemed able to give us any definite reason why there should be a quarantine, or indeed if there was a quarantine. Sure enough an emphatic, expressionless face gave us the order and kept our passports. We asked, 'why?' 'Because you've been to Iraq and they have cholera.' 'But we've had five days quarantine to go into Jordan.' 'Your passports will in returned in five days.' There was no point in pursuing this particular path. 'Can you please direct us to your quarantine campsite.' 'We have no campsite, but we have no one in our hospital so you may stay there.' Then almost as an afterthought, 'And you must not walk into the town during your confinement, so the doctor will get you food.' The doctor couldn't have been more pleasant, he welcomed us with open arms. All this really was getting quite surreal. It was as though we were in a disjointed film where the director had no idea of the plot. This hospital wasn't a couple of rooms pretending to be a hospital, it really was a hospital. It had wards, all full of hospital beds, and shower rooms off the wards, and even an equipped operating theatre. How there could be 'no patients' in a reasonably sized town such as this, was not believable. Unless of course, they'd found the answer to life. We chatted to the Doctor about his work in the town and chose our ward for our five-day stay. Nothing seemed amiss. But what did become apparent quite quickly, was the same problem we had from the very beginning. My two girls. Which one was free? He asked us what sort of food we'd like and kindly offered to bring it himself. The time passed quite pleasantly really, with the doctor's daily visits and very long chats. He was well read, spoke English almost flawlessly and was very interesting about the politics of the country. On the evening of the third day, he brought our supper as usual, but this time with a bottle of red wine. We glanced at one another. He was about to make his move. Supper went on and on and he stayed and stayed, the last drop of red wine had been squeezed from the bottle. What on earth were we to do. Our saviour suddenly arrived in the form of a roar of an engine, screeching to a halt outside the hospital front door. We thankfully flew to the windows, only to see a filthy dark-green Jaguar car that had evidently lost its exhaust. All four doors flung open simultaneously and out jumped five of the scruffiest young men you'd see anywhere. One of them younger than the others, probably about nineteen, and the driver a bit older with a short ginger beard, the other three in their midtwenties. The Doctor was furious. His evening ruined, he threw himself out of the ward and down the stairs to the front door. Shouting orders at the bewildered five young men, he turned on his heel and flounced off down the hill and back to the town. We introduced ourselves to our new companions, telling them how well we'd been treated and remarkably, the food was on the house. However, no food and no doctor appeared again. We wondered what would happen at the end of our confinement. We needn't have worried, on the morning we were due to leave, the doctor arrived with our passports and returned them with a smile and a little bow. We shook hands and he wished us well for the rest of our trip. No hint of embarrassment or awkwardness of why we hadn't seen him after he flounced off when the new intake arrived; or why the food so abruptly ceased to materialise after being so abundant for the first half of our quarantine. I can only suppose we were considered 'fair game', some you win, some you lose.

A little episode happened with the group of young men; I seem to be talking about them as though they were younger than me. whereas the older one, the one with the ginger beard was, in fact, older. It turned out they were very short of money. I've no idea how they thought they'd get to England. The evening of the day before we were due to leave, I went to check everything was in order with the car. I couldn't believe my eyes when I glanced at the fuel gauge. Then stared at it in disbelief. It was completely empty. I checked with the girls we'd filled the tank just before leaving Jordan. There was only one conclusion, all the petrol had been siphoned out. After a brief discussion, I had no alternative but to confront the boys. The elder one hung his head in shame, and the others shuffled about, hands in pockets, looking at their shoes. He gave me the cash for the petrol. I'd like to have said 'you can keep it' but we weren't in the position for such generosity.

In the morning we set forth for Damascus, leaving behind five young men, who'd be our age now, and who we'd neither see nor hear of again. And a doctor, with an empty hospital, who'd 'tried-it-on' and failed. If all these disparate little episodes add up to make a life, no wonder our dreams are so diverse and confusing when everything we've ever done is recorded in such detail.

I think I've briefly told you about Damascus, and as I don't want this part of my story to turn into a travelogue I'll just reiterate one thing I remember most vividly. We were told by our self-appointed guide that there would be a war, in three or four months from then, between all the surrounding countries with adjacent borders to Israel, to reinstate the Palestinian Nation to its rightful position on the map of the world, which did not include the state of Israel. At the time, I didn't realise the enormous relevance of what we were told. Why were we, three very young travellers, told something of such incredible significance to all that's happening in the Middle East to this day? How could I have not taken it in? Here was an opportunity, handed to us on a plate, for a thoughtful discussion. Was this man an Arab or a Jew? What did he do? What was his purpose? Where did he live? How did he make his living? So much we could have talked about. He was with us for most of the day. We were worried he would ask us for money, but he didn't. C wanted to go to the street called Straight. He took us there. She bought yet another gown she still wears to this day. It's made of bright white, beautifully embroidered, soft cotton with long sleeves and hangs to the ground. A man's actually, but she wears it well. The hundreds of little narrow streets of silversmiths were beautiful and dazzling. I wish I could go today with, at least 'some' money, but the civil war makes it impossible.

After a few days, we tore ourselves away from this enticing city and made our way to another lovely city, Beirut, the capital of the Lebanon. It's hardly possible to reconcile the city now and the city then. I haven't been back since we were there in 1965, but the newsreel footage and journalist-word-painting, depict it as a comparable hellhole. My father would describe to me the attractiveness, the interest, the pleasure that was Mogadishu in Somalia. Antique shops full of beautiful furniture, pictures, and jewellery, restaurants with all manner of food, one after another, along the seafront. Beirut became a similar contradiction.

Our campsite, called Aamchit, a mile or two north of the city, was beautifully positioned on a rocky outcrop on the edge of the Mediterranean. I've tried to look for it on Google Earth, but it no longer exists as a campsite, the position would now be too valuable. The facilities all beautifully clean, even hot water in the showers, and the restaurant serving delicious cheap food, making it unnecessary to prepare our own. Beirut itself was a beautiful vibrant, but calm city. We wandered about, stopping at street cafes whenever we wished, ambling through the old town, winding our way along narrow, fascinating little streets, filled with every manner of shops you can envisage. Every doorway offered a warm, friendly, smiling, welcoming face, inviting us in for a glass of tea and a chat. If we didn't want to buy anything, there was never any pressure to do so. They, in their turn, were amazed to hear we'd left Mombasa harbour and were driving all the way back from Kuwait to London. Other days we just stayed at our campsite, sunbathing on the flat-topped rocks and diving into the crystal clear, azure blue, Mediterranean Sea to cool off. Inevitably, if Honey ever made the mistake of swimming on her own, within a blink of an eye, as if from nowhere, a slinky motor launch would silently sidle alongside and she'd be invited aboard for a drink. All the well bronzed men, in their early forties, with black, greased-back hair, with a hint of grey at the temples, never seemed to mind very much when she accepted, but only if her friends could come aboard with her. Many a pleasant afternoon, after a Lebanese Mezze lunch, swilled down with a cold bottle of local dry white wine, was spent aboard very expensive motor launches. We visited all the places you'd expect should be visited; The Cedars of Lebanon, the ancient columns of Baalbek, Byblos, and further up the coast, beautiful long white beaches, nothing like it is today. The vineyards, the mountains, the Sea, Lebanon is such a beautiful country. Only three tiny months later, after the Six-day-War, did the illusion of calm, throughout the Middle East, begin to erupt into the seething caldron of hatred and destruction that is the whole of the Middle East today. We were caught up in the illusion of calm and stayed too long indulging in the tranquillity and ease of life in which we, so unexpectedly, found ourselves. Our indulgence was compounded by the two weeks of enforced quarantine on the two borders, into Jordan and Syria. We wouldn't pay for the mistake for another six weeks or so, when trying to cross the Austrian Alps on one of the highest, smallest passes, in six feet of snow. Our car had no heating, and was built for hot, African dusty roads! If we had known, I don't think we would have been able to tear ourselves away anyway. After all, everything we were doing, from the day we left Mombasa harbour, was a one-off, so all we experienced was to be savoured and made the very most of.

After a few more days we were ready to set forth. It felt as though we were leaving home, starting afresh. We drove north in the car which had been packed with all we might need for any more enforced lengthy stays at other border crossings. We reluctantly left the prettiest, warmest most pleasant people of all the countries we'd been through so far, and crossed the border back into Syria.

Without thinking about it, I'd done all the driving so far. It was never tiring because we never had to hurry to be anywhere in particular at any particular time. In retrospect, that whole trip, except for the last two days, from Hamburg to London, must have been the most trouble free four months I've ever had, for almost my entire life. Only now, as I write this in my seventy-first year, am I, once again, at peace in myself and in my surroundings. But getting here was to be a tortuous journey. A journey an awful lot of people throughout the world must despairingly, have to suffer. I've suddenly jumped a long way ahead. So back to driving, unhurriedly, through the villages of Syria, waving to smiling faces, stopping for coffees and our morning prepared lunches, there wasn't a worry in the world. How wrong we were and how terrifyingly different it is now. We stopped and pitched our tent in the friendly little city of Homs and then in Aleppo.

We're not shown, on any of the newsflashes on the television about the war in Syria, what the centres of the cities look like. If the devastation wrought upon the outskirts is anything to go by, those cities will have to be completely rebuilt. And I don't think that will happen in our lifetime. I suppose there must have been an undercurrent of unrest wherever we went, but as young travellers, we weren't aware of the awfulness that was to befall those lovely Middle Eastern countries, as we so contentedly meandered through them.

Honey had a contact in the British Embassy in Ankara in Turkey, so that was a vague goal. It took a few days of zigzagging about from the border with Syria, but we found ourselves arriving quite late one evening in the outskirts of Ankara. We tried to make it a rule not to arrive after dark at any destination and try to find somewhere to pitch our tent. But this time, as with quite a few other times, we were again looking for the campsite well after dark. Needless to say, we couldn't find it. Searching about, lost, we came across a deserted, derelict building site. We forced our way in through padlocked gates by taking one side off its hinges. We found an ideal spot on one of the concrete floors covered by the next floor up, so we didn't have to erect our little tent. We looked out on to a pool of darkness with street lights shining in the distance. The daylight would bring us the view. We rolled out our sleeping bags and after a satisfying Turkish type supper cooked on our two-burner gas cooker, we climbed into them and went out for the count.

When I think back, living in this modern comfort everyone expects today, it seems extraordinary we should have chosen to put ourselves through such discomfort without a second thought of the danger that might have befallen us. At no point, during the four months we were travelling, pitching our tent anywhere at the end of the day, did we think we might be in any sort of danger.

The early morning sunlight brought us a splendid view of a well laid-out park of trees, running in avenues between man-made lakes with bright green mown lawns flowing down to the water's edge. The whole city stretched out beyond. We silently stared out, open-mouthed. We looked at each other and smiled.

Honey's Ambassador invited us to dinner. All very smart, everything you'd expect from somebody in that position. Although it was only a relatively short time since we'd left our homes, we'd got used to the standard of living into which we'd put ourselves, due to our limited budget. So the difference between 'us-and-them' was very accentuated and made for interesting discussion, not with them, but later on between ourselves. We told them about our beautiful view on waking up, but we refrained from telling them about our actual choice of living arrangements. The evening flowed along very smoothly, the conversation never flagged, they were, after all, real pros, entertaining is part of the brief. But by the end of the evening, when we shook hands to say goodbye, I think we left a very baffled couple.

I regret not visiting any of the little towns and villages along the Black Sea, but Honey had done a lot of reading about the ancient city of Ephesus so was eagerly awaiting our arrival there. In fact, ever since crossing the border into Turkey, she could hardly talk about anything else. So we wound our way south-west and, this time, arriving before darkness engulfed, we found the campsite.

I must say it was intriguing, no, much more than intriguing, staggering, or any other superlative you can come up with. How such a city could even be conceived such a long time ago, especially when now, with all our modern technology, we surround something like that, with dreadful concrete blocks. They have no merit, no sense of history, no design, nothing commendable in any way. It's as though we've taken a step into darkness and we're still falling. I suppose it could be said, that now, nearly fifty years later, our sense of design, in a very broad sense, is beginning to formulate itself again. We do sometimes build things of wonder. But not entire cities. I'm sure the people living in the Ephesus then, would have thought their city was something worthy of wonder.

There weren't many people wandering about. Looking at the photographs we took then, we were the only ones in them. While walking about within the whole site we couldn't say much to each other, there seemed to be an immense enveloping presence. Even back at the campsite, we quietly went about our duties, preparing and cooking our food, laying out the sleeping bags, washing and soundly sleeping, waking at the crack of dawn.

Istanbul. What a city. The sprawl around all cities wasn't so prominent a feature at that time. I don't really remember it spoiling the enjoyment and excitement of our arrival at such an historical, beautiful, yet modern and vibrant a city. The traffic wasn't too heavy, so we could easily dawdle about, without being hooted at too much, wondering at all the sites without worrying if we were lost, which of course we were.

The campsite turned out to be some miles from the city centre, but well laid-out with good amenities and a cheap restaurant. We settled in very easily and quickly and as was the norm by now, our fellow-travellers were immediately friendly and communicative, swapping stories and describing places they'd been. We were advised to dispense with the car for going in and out of the city, and instead to use the local yellow taxis, which were far more cost-effective. You'd stand on any main road and flag one down and if they had any room they'd stop and we'd squeeze in. We could then get out anywhere along their route, which depended on where the furthest passenger wanted to go; in turn our route might become the furthest, so we'd each have to pay accordingly.

There was so much to see and do. If we'd suddenly been given the opportunity to stay six months in or around that city, I think we'd have jumped at it. The Topkapi Palace, The Blue Mosque, Hagia Sophia, all so magnificent, majestic, astounding in their very concept. But the place we enjoyed the most, because of its vibrancy and essence of thrumming life, was the Grand Bazaar. It drew us back on a number of occasions. But the outstanding memory, apart from little trinkets we still have, were the great cauldrons of steaming Turkish peasant foods lined up along the walls of the entrance to the Bazaar. We were always hungry and so the tastes and smells and sheer deliciousness of the contents of those cauldrons, remain with me to this day. Tastes and smells are so evocative they take you back and forth in an instant.

Another time, in another life, my Sister and I were in Paris together, with no money. Not just a tiny amount of money, I mean no money and we didn't speak any useful French to get some work. It seemed our only option was to write home to say we were starving. I think my father would have said, 'I've been starving hungry and I had no one to turn to, so let them work it out for themselves. My mother immediately sent us enough money to at least eat for a few days, and for me to get back to London. The smell of that plate of the cheapest food we could find, will be in my senses forever.

We weren't at that stage yet, but the very cheapest option always had to be the final choice. Sometimes it was very difficult to decide which of the cheapest options to choose, presuming we'd never be in this particular position again. So here, our choice was something the local residents took for granted. We hopped on to the ferry that ploughed up and down the Bosporus from the city to the Black Sea. We stayed on-board at each destination going back and forth three or four times. As long as we stayed on-board we didn't have to pay again. The ticket collector laughed, 'Not you three again, but we like it that you like us so much.'

It was with heavy hearts we reluctantly began to realise we must be on the move again. Although we still had a long way to go, I think we all sensed, when leaving Istanbul, it would be the beginning of the end of our lackadaisical travelling. Packing up the car was a laborious business. It had never been a chore before, and it took the whole day. To give ourselves a bit of a lift, we decided to squeeze ourselves into one of those yellow cabs, and go back to the entrance to the Grand Bazaar. We'd have a delicious supper, one more time, from those steaming, bubbling cauldrons lined against the wall on the way in. There was never any chance of wine or even beer, a huge factor now, and bottled water had yet to flood into all our lives. The only thing we ever drank, away from our little tent, was scalding hot tea.

Early the following morning we shook hands with our fellow-travellers and wished each other well for the remainder of our journeys. Some had a long, long way to go, not planning to stop for another year or so.

For us though, crossing the Turkish border into Northern Greece was an emotional moment. We turned off the main road and drove to the top of a hill. I stopped the engine. We got out and silently stood, looking back at Turkey, and brought to mind all we'd done in only the past three months. Now, as I write this, fifty years later, trawling my memory banks, I cannot recall a harsh word ever spoken between us. And as far as C's parents were concerned, Honey was the most vigilant of chaperones.

How it was possible for the three of us to live so intimately, for more than three months, with not a harsh word spoken, in such a confined space for all that time, I really don't know. It's not as though we were the same in any way. Our backgrounds, our upbringings were all completely different. It might have been because we were so fond of one another, or it might have been for fear of the consequences of not getting along. Whichever it was, we stood quietly, leaning up against our faithful little Toyota Corona Estate, with hundreds of thousands of miles on the clock. We looked back into the misty haze of Turkey, and earlier, since leaving the port of Mombasa, and smiled at each other with a sense of achievement. Ideally, the whole trip should have ended here. Not that the possibility of doing so even entered our minds, but the Middle East and Europe are so different, each are separate entities to be appreciated in their own right.

It was now coming towards the end of November and Europe was definitely beginning to shroud itself with its winter blanket. We, on the other hand, had nothing of the sort. Even the poor car didn't have any heating. It was only by chance when filling with petrol, the pump attendant casually asked, 'Shall I top-up the antifreeze?'

I'm talking as though we were driving directly into Europe as it is now, but then, of course, we still had the immensity of Yugoslavia through which to wend our way. One day, after a very pleasant night stop, we drove down a little track off the main road, and into what once could have been an orchard, the ancient, gnarled trees were mesmerizingly beautiful. I turned off the engine. It was perfectly quiet and still. All the trees must have stood there for hundreds of years. They had a presence silently standing there in perfect stillness. We didn't say anything. We slowly got out of the car and wandered about, gently touching the trunks with the palm of our hands, as though they were magnificent animals.

Just recently we were taken, by Gwynne (who so memorably had carried me out to the reef), into a game park in Tanzania. He stopped the Land Rover to let a herd of elephants cross the road in front of us. The herd must have been over a hundred strong. They slowly began to surround the car. I could feel my heart thumping in my chest. We shouldn't be here. One elephant stopped right next to my window. He slowly turned his head and looked at me. I caught his eye. We stared at one another. Through his huge, dense, black eye, perfectly surrounded with long beautiful eyelashes any woman would die for, it seemed as though I was looking through a window deep into his soul. Surely he must have heard my heart crashing against my ribs. Only seconds later he quietly turned away. The whole herd disregarding us, went about their business, pulling up great bunches of newly grown, long, lush green grass that springs to life after hard, heavy savannah rains.

Being there, in that orchard, with no one else around, among all those knowing old trees, was very similar, without the thumping heart, to being in the middle of that great herd of majestic elephants. An incredible sensation.

Later the following morning we stopped to fill the car with fuel and have a coffee. A man with the similar mission as ourselves, parked himself at our table and immediately launched into conversation as though he knew us. We were used to this sort of thing happening quite often because of the unerring magnet of my two girls. After a torrent of questions, in almost perfect English, he said, 'Well, if you want my advice,' for which we weren't aware we'd asked, 'you should take time to drive through Yugoslavia. Fairly soon, certainly in your lifetime, there will be a deadly eruption in that country that will change it forever. You might never have the chance to go there again.' We didn't know what to say, we just looked at him. It was the second time we'd been given almost exactly the same sort of information by the man I told you about earlier in Damascus. Only that had been about Israel and its war with its Arab neighbours.

He was absolutely correct in all respects. Yugoslavia no longer exists, it was a deadly, terrible eruption that tore the whole country apart, back into its original states before Tito artificially created Yugoslavia.

We took his advice to a certain degree, zigzagging away from our main route, taking a few extra days pitching our tent in farmers' fields, briefly visiting the beautiful cities everyone's heard about. Although we never felt unsafe, because of the warm welcome from practically everyone we met, and to which we'd grown accustomed wherever we travelled, we did have an awareness of an undercurrent of unrest here, that made us feel uncomfortable. From area to area, even though we didn't understand anything spoken, there was a palpable difference in attitude. We should have known more, of course, but now we know the ignorance of youth is always astonishing.

We crossed the border into Austria at a point that lead us to the most direct route over the Alps, into Germany and straight on to the autobahn pointing north to Hamburg. This may sound straightforward, but crossing the Alps at that time of the year, through one of the smallest, highest passes on the map, perhaps wasn't the best of decisions. We could clearly see all the heavy snow shrouding the mountains ahead, but we thought that as the pass was open, it was obviously passable. It was passable, but only for 4x4's with studded tyres or chains and proper heating inside, whereas our poor little African car had nothing suitable for the vagaries ahead. Quite soon, on leaving the border, the road started to ascend. The snow quickly piled thicker and thicker on the side of the road. The road itself became white with un-melted snow. I stopped the car, 'Perhaps we should stay on the main roads and take the tunnel under the mountains rather than climbing over the mountains.' Surprisingly, both girls said, 'No, no we've just driven through the whole of the Middle East and Turkey, we can't let a little snow defeat us.' I said, 'If this is a little snow, what's a lot of snow?' They both said, 'It'll be exciting.' The majority vote won. Very surprisingly, without much skidding about, we did make incredibly good headway. We were so proud of our sturdy little African car. Quite suddenly the road started to descend. We looked at each other and laughed at our achievement. Too soon! I touched the brakes. No response. I touched them again. Still no response. A shaft of ice ran itself through the middle of my body. What can I do? I changed gear down to second, then again to first, the response was minimal. A stationary car was fast coming up ahead. What could I do? I couldn't steer around it, into oncoming traffic, I couldn't see beyond it. The only alternative was to crash the car into my side of the icy bank. The ice was so hard it wouldn't let me in. The car ahead was looming closer and closer. I steered into the bank again. The noise of the bumper tearing against the ice was awful. I'd started to slow down. But not enough. I crashed into the car in front, bumper-to-bumper. I can still hear that noise now. The driver flung his door open, he descended on us, his face swollen purple with rage. I couldn't get out, my door was jammed closed by the wall of ice on the left. My girls, meanwhile, were struck dumb with the horror of what was befalling us, so soon after laughing with pleasure, when reaching the top of the pass. It turned out there wasn't much damage done, apart from dented bumpers, and the driver himself had had to do the same thing to stop his own car.

As luck would have it, a hundred yards ahead, on the right-hand side, was an inn. An Austrian Chalet Inn, with three feet of snow on the roof. We slid, like a crab, down the hill, as the queue of cars ahead cleared, and tentatively crept into the car park. How could there be a room in which to lay our weary heads? Not only was there a room, it had three separate beds with an enormous, puffed-up duvet on each. And better still, the night under these inviting duvets included a delicious supper with a carafe of wine. Also, our sturdy little African car was not forgotten. It was allowed into the barn, with the cows to keep it warm. It couldn't feel more at home.

In the morning, the proprietors wouldn't let us leave, to slide sideways down the rest of the pass. They ordered a huge 4x4 lorry, specially built for this particular purpose, to come and escort us down the remainder of the pass. With a great deal of kissing and shaking of hands, we bade our farewells. The driver of the lorry was a cheery chap who knew exactly what he was doing. He attached a tow rope to our rear axle, and the other end was attached to the front of his gigantic lorry with enormous studded balloon tires, to fix the lorry to any surface. With the power and size of that vehicle, I think he could have climbed a mountain face.

I was instructed to drive slowly ahead of him until I started to slip, then to put the gearbox into neutral and turn off the engine. He would then determine the speed of the descent, and I would steer as tightly as I could on the right of the road. On no account was I ever, ever to touch the brake pedal. If I did, and he knew how tempting that would be to do so, I would lose control of the steering and I would dangle about in front of him like a worm held by its tail. His treat would be my girls with him in his spacious, warm cab. All was going well until about halfway down. The road was becoming steeper and steeper, and instead of slowing, he was driving faster and faster. It felt as though he'd lost control, that question hadn't arisen in his instructions. My brake peddle leg had a will of its own. Ever since I'd learnt to drive all those years ago, if I needed to slow-down in any situation I would use the brakes. Now I needed to slow down, not go faster, but not use my brakes. I desperately looked in the mirror. He wasn't even looking at me. He and my girls all had their heads thrown back in open-mouthed laughter. A momentary rage brought my right leg back into my control. At the bottom of the pass when the road had flattened, he stopped his vehicle and quickly climbed out of his cab. Before I could say anything, he said, 'I'm very sorry I didn't tell you I would be going faster on the steeper parts of the road, to keep you in my control, I don't know how you kept your foot off the brakes.' I didn't say, 'I thought you were enjoying yourself a bit too much.'

We all happily shook hands and we sped off north to Hamburg. We only had one more night together. We'd done and seen so much. We'd lived so intimately. Honey had undertaken her task of chaperone admirably.

We couldn't afford anywhere splendid, we were down to our last few shekels as it was. The autobahn motel served very well, but the poor little car couldn't cope with the cold, and froze solid overnight. The poor thing had to be warmed-up, with hot air fans, in the nearby garage, before it showed any sign of life. Late that afternoon Honey directed us through miles of modern, tidy, orderly neighbourhoods, back into her life, she'd left behind a lifetime ago. We were down-in-the-mouth and monosyllabic.

In the morning C and I made our 24-hour non-stop drive back to our lives in England.

Back to London

I'd never been in a good enough financial position to be married, but that rather vital factor didn't seem to worry me in the least. When I asked C's father if I could marry his daughter he asked me how I thought I'd support her. I said, 'If I'm lucky I might make as much as £1000 a year.' He was hard of hearing, so he asked me to repeat what I'd just said. He'd heard me the first time, but he couldn't believe what he'd heard. He, very hesitantly said, 'I think you'll need a little more than that. Please could you wait a while.' But his 'while' and my 'while' were a long way apart. I simplistically thought if two people loved each other they should live together and make a life together. Marriage was a formality. What could be plainer than that?

The acting profession is really in a category of its own. You're either in work or you're not. If not, you still remain an actor but you're not acting. In 1966, I don't remember it ever being difficult to find some sort of job at a moment's notice.

On returning to London after our honeymoon in Kenya, and a few days in Paris, we had nowhere to come back to. Even that fact didn't worry me in the least. We'd been given the use of a flat in central London by C's baffled, elderly uncle, for a few weeks. So it was from there we set forth to find a home. It took longer than I'd hoped, but we did find a small two bedroom flat on the Edgware Road just up from Marble Arch with which we were very pleased.

But I've jumped ahead of myself. I'll go back to the beginning of the time we'd arrived back in London after our mammoth non-stop drive from Hamburg.

It was almost exactly a year since I was introduced to C's family, and then getting married. C's mother had had a nervous breakdown from the effect of us driving back to England together, albeit with a chaperone. So I was somewhat apprehensive about my initial introduction. She couldn't have been more civil. She came straight up to me, shook me by the hand and said, 'so, at last we meet.' I was very lucky.

Before leaving Nairobi, C had a job as a programme presenter with The Voice of Kenya radio. She took to it like a duck to water and loved doing it in the same way I loved to be in a theatre. So she applied to the BBC for the job of 'studio manager'. She was with them for about 18 months. It was because she worked at the BBC, she wanted to be married at All Souls Langham Place, the BBC church. For the banns to be read, I had to be living in that parish. It would be deemed as living at an address if I had a suitcase with a few clothes in it for the three weeks they were read. I rang a number in the Evening Standard newspaper that advertised rooms and put forward my plight. Without a second thought the landlord agreed, technically that suitcase is still there.

During the year leading up to the wedding, C was working at the BBC and I was doing all sorts of jobs, some acting and some definitely not. I was, of course, aware that I had no money other than what I earned for day-to-day living. Even I began to think perhaps I wasn't suitable material for marriage. No prospects, nothing.

One of the auditions I attended was at a public swimming pool at the top of Shaftesbury Avenue in London. There must have been at least fifty of us out-of-work actors huddled about the pool wearing swimming trunks. We were being auditioned for four non-speaking parts, in a little film called Submarine X1, introducing an up-and-coming, possible Hollywood Star, called James Caen. We were all told to jump in to prove we could swim. Quite extraordinary how many of them had no idea what to do when in water. A couple of them even had to be 'saved' by the pool guard. The rest of us were then sorted into groups of similar height. Three at a time we then jumped in again and were told to hold our breath, on the bottom of the pool, for as long as possible. I was in my element. I couldn't help showing off by holding my breath on the bottom for so long they had to send a guard in to see if I was in trouble. After another couple of hours of being told to do the most absurd antics you can possibly think of, they'd whittled us down to about ten people. By now we were quite cold, hugging our own bodies to try to keep warm.

I found myself suddenly transported back to my childhood, to the years I attended my prep school in Kenya near Eldoret. Every morning queues of pathetic shivering, skinny white bodies, hugging themselves endeavouring to keep warm, while waiting for the basins of brown cold water. Making an attempt to wash, before hurriedly dressing, only to stand in another queue for our skimpy breakfast of solid porridge and a hard-boiled egg. All the memories must be so sharp because others around the same time are so joyful. The joy of running to the stables to say good morning to my beloved Thistle, already saddled up, whinnying when he saw me, then gliding through the countryside with his long smooth strides.

Back to the swimming pool in central London, so different yet linked to a beautiful crisp, clear picture. One must be grateful for small mercies. We were summarily dismissed and told in an offhand manner, our agents may or may not be in touch. I wonder why it's so prevalent when people who are given temporary authority over others, are so rude. I skulked back to my lonely one room abode, stinking of chlorine, and ran myself a hot bath to wash it all away. After a few days the memory of the pool, C working long hours at the BBC and me going hither and thither from job to job and audition to audition, began to recede. As an actor, you feel as though you can't ever be far from a telephone. The next ring is bound to be your agent lining up an excellent offer for the lead in a play for which you're about to audition. However, he did ring, but it wasn't for the lead in a play, the Submarine X1 producer wanted to see me at their offices in Elstree. My mind went haywire, my heart beat so hard I thought it would jump out of my chest. On arrival at their offices, I was given the script. This was getting better and better. The producer was a very small-framed man, an American, with a round pallid face and black slicked down hair, sitting behind an enormous desk. He asked me to read a few lines. Then he said. 'Your part hasn't got any lines and he's killed at the beginning of the film, we just want to make sure you can act as a fallback. Thanks for coming, we'll be in touch.' Can you imagine the let-down? I think you can. But I stood up, beamed my gratitude for seeing me, shook him warmly by the hand and left the office. A few days later my agent was given the offer; £70 a day for seven days, on location in Scotland on Loch Ness.

The reason why I'm taking such a long time telling you, in such detail, about this minuscule episode that happened about fifty years ago, is because with the presentation of that cheque from the producers of Submarine X1, I said to C and her father, 'Surely you can't have any doubts now I can support a wife.' Pathetic when I think back.

The wedding was planned for the first of December 1967, my father-in-law's birthday. Why we thought I would be a good birthday present, I'm not entirely sure. It was quite a grand affair for then. There were about two hundred people at the church and the hymns were very carefully chosen by C with her love of music, and the choir sang a beautiful anthem 'Love one another'. The vicar taking our service was quite a well-known clergyman called John Stott. He died very recently. He was a stickler for time and he told C she must not be more than five minutes late. He'd be there waiting on the steps. Five minutes came and went, ten minutes came and went, fifteen, twenty. A taxi suddenly rushed into view and screeched to a halt at the bottom of the church steps. A baffled vicar stood at the top not knowing what to do. The taxi door opened and inside, filling the whole cab, was a mass of snow-white wedding dress, veil and train, billowing to be let out. Also with C, somewhere hidden by the white snow, was her father and their assistant who, once on the pavement, straightened C's dress and laid out the train. She was ushered to the top of the steps to an agitated but relieved vicar. Her two little unruly nephews were the pages, and true to form they ran around the church shouting for their mothers. She held her father's arm and they walked slowly up the aisle in time to the wedding march, he reluctantly gave her to me and I could see her beauty shining through her veil.

It turned out, the reason why she was so late, was because the car due to bring her from their club to the church had not been ordered. She was all dressed standing in the courtyard of the club, with her father, when they suddenly realised. The doorman had to run out into Piccadilly and hail a taxi. The driver understood the emergency and legitimately had the fun of tearing about jumping all the lights.

It was a lovely service and we had it all recorded on tape. I was quite nervous so I spoke too fast. I'd been nervous going on stage, of course, but I had a character to hide behind, and everything was well rehearsed. This was just us, a one-off, the most important ceremony in which we'd ever take part.

In those days it wasn't expected that the whole congregation, after the ceremony itself, would be given a lavish three-course, sit-down meal, with as much wine and champagne to supply a cruise liner for a month. Not to mention an enormous marquee more suitable for the King of Saudi Arabia. Instead the congregation would quietly gather at *one's club*, in our case, the Naval and Military in Piccadilly, have a couple of glasses of champagne, a sandwich or two, then cake and speeches. A change of clothing for the bride and groom, and the wave-off. So much more dignified.

My mother-in-law had lent us her beautiful Daimler for me to drive to the airport. We picked up my wife's Cousin Peter at the other side of the underpass at Hyde Park Corner, for him to drive the car back to the club.

We flew to Paris and spent two lovely, serene days in a little homely hotel just off the Champs Elysees. We had nothing to do but wander about the city. Wonderful. It was strange we knew each other so well but had never spent a night together, or with anyone else. I wouldn't have thought that situation could ever exist today, or ever again.

***

I told you earlier I was assistant stage manager (ASM) /actor, with the Donovan Maule Theatre in Nairobi. I'd turned down their offer to remain with them, in the expectation of furthering my career by returning to London. Well, ten years later I'd achieved absolutely nothing.

I still maintain, if you're not making a living in your chosen profession after ten years, you should do something else. If you love doing it, whatever it is, you can still be part of it but you must make your living and earn enough money to support your way of life. So reluctantly, I realised I was in the same position as many other actors, in fact, the majority by far, of not earning enough money from acting to support my wife and myself.

One of the few jobs I had, and enjoyed the most, was being part of the Royal Shakespeare Company at the Aldwych Theatre in London for a year. Although in a very lowly position, it did include a tour around Europe. I was asked by an actor who'd remained with the Donovan Maule Theatre in Nairobi all his working life, what had I been doing for the last year. I said, rather grandly, I'd been with the R.S.C. He looked at me in utter astonishment and said 'You've been in the Irish Sea. What on earth were you doing in the Irish Sea?'

Being part of that Company was a lovely experience. In repertory we played, Troilus & Cressida, Revengers Tragedy, and Bartholomew Fair. I suppose there may have been about forty of us altogether in that one company. Before they became household names were, Norman Rodway, Michael Williams, whose voice as Troilus, boomed out so musically every time he spoke, Ian Richardson, Alan Howard, Patrick Stewart and Helen Mirren. They were regarded as good actors, but no more so than anyone else. No hint of the stars they were to become. Fascinating watching them grow into the roles they now hold, thrust upon them by the viewing public.

It was obvious, to me at least, I had to change my way of earning a living. We'd recently been back to see my parents in Kenya, and a long-standing friend of mine since prep school, couldn't understand that if we wanted a new way of life, why look any further than where I used to live. My father would give me as much land as I would need for doing anything I wanted to do, we could build ourselves a house and start afresh.

Living in London with not enough money is no fun. The call of the wild grew to a crescendo. I don't know why, but we never discussed this change of direction definitively, as something my wife may or may not want to do. I can only excuse myself by saying, we were, and still are, so bound-up with one another, living in each other's pockets, I just assumed she knew what I was thinking. After all, she did go along with the whole plan. We were driven to the airport by my Uncle and Aunt, and as my little wife kissed my Aunt goodbye, tears rolled down her cheeks. It's a picture, a snapshot that has always stayed with me.

***

My wife had come into a small sum of money, on her twenty-first birthday, her father had made over to her as a child. It had then grown into a sum large enough to buy a small, run-down Georgian terraced house, in a square just off Clapham Common, in South London. Her mother was horrified. Once again her beautiful daughter had been led into doing something so far away from her expectations. Then, I discarded her sentiments as being out-of-date and worthless. Now, looking back, I'm embarrassed and ashamed at my brainless attitude and general lack of care and understanding for someone who merely loved her daughter and genuinely feared for her well-being.

The whole square was council tenanted and a developer bought it as a speculation for next to nothing. He then came to individual financial arrangements with each tenant to either leave completely or move to other houses within the square. As each house became vacant, he'd put it freehold on to a fast-rising house market. It was a very good ruse for him and it was a very good investment for us.

In 1971, after a last-minute gazump from his lawyers, and much to the embarrassment of ours, we acquired it for £11,500. It was a very neat little house, but it was very little. A half basement with two small rooms, one front and one back, the same upstairs and the same on the first floor, then there was the roof space. One cold water tap and no indoor loo. It's incredible that so recently as 1971, people, in our capital city of London, one of the most renowned cities in the world, had to live in conditions such as those. We spoke to the previous tenants while doing the renovations and they seemed completely accepting of their situation. Yes, it was very cold in the winter, yes, there was only one cold water tap, and yes, they had to venture outside to get to the loo all the year round, but that's all there was on offer. No hint of resentment, or wishing they could afford a house of their own. They were tenants, and that's all tenants were offered. It's difficult to comprehend, the sweeping change in mindset that would have to happen when, only a few years later, Mrs Thatcher would come into power.

While all the alterations took place, we really needed to be on-site as I was acting as site manager and every night we needed somewhere to lay our weary heads. The new terms of our tenancy for the flat we lived in on the Edgware Road just up from Marble Arch, had caused us to buy the house in the first place. I swapped our car, our little faithful, Toyota Estate that had served us so well all way from Kuwait to London, for a scooter to take us around London. Also, an old Bedford Van that had been a mobile shop, and which I planned to convert into a mobile home. I did rebuild it into a mobile home, and a very smart mobile home it was too. Looking at the photographs now, of all the work I must have done to build it into a state we could live in I just don't know how I thought I could do it. Water, cooker, shower, loo, double bed, dining table, cupboards, everything a modern mobile home would have, only I did it myself. Anyway we did it and we parked it outside our newly acquired little house. We lived in it while we ripped out the inside, and rebuilt it into a very smart, fully equipped, modern, two bedroom house. Then we added an extension into the garden at the back for the kitchen come dining room. We created a separate one bedroom flat in the half basement for an income, not much of an income, but an income.

One of the little teams of people we used to build more drains and access manholes were two particularly helpful and pleasant rather overweight middle-aged men. They had a fund of knowledge, not only to do with house building, but a whole range of subjects. During their tea breaks we could talk about anything, so I wondered why they were building drains for a living. Not that drain building isn't a very necessary and skilful thing to do well, but nevertheless I thought they could do better. I found myself looking forward to our chats at morning tea, lunch and afternoon tea. Slowly it began to emerge, they'd grown up as close mates on the same street, they'd been to the same school, they'd married the girls next door. While sitting around evening after evening talking about what they wanted to achieve, and all the things they'd like to do with their lives, they began to realise, that from their background, there was such a small chance of getting anywhere. They must accept their lot or do something that would make a lot of money quickly. But what? Slowly, a flicker of an idea began to emerge at the back of their minds. They couldn't say who actually thought of it because it was such a dim, faraway light in the distance. It became brighter as they unknowingly got closer and closer. Then, suddenly, it was there, a brilliant, beaming lighthouse, showing the way. They would become professional criminals. They had friends who were making quite a good living. The risk, of course, was getting caught and going to gaol. They weighed up the pros and cons and came to the conclusion with the potential gains the risks were worth taking. One really big one and they could retire. The morality of the decision didn't figure, even when I posed it as an idea, they just looked baffled. 'So why did you stop?' 'We were in prison for the fird time, and the sentences were getin' longer and longer. We were sitin' opposite each uver, splitin' a match in two, and we look up at each uver, and almost togever said, this ain't working is it? We decided to stop and go straight.' So they learnt a trade while in prison, which was how they were here now.

Towards the end of their contract, I got an offer of a small part on a series called 'The Regiment'. The tiny scene was to be shot in Morocco, as it required a Boer, *me*, being captured by the British while galloping across the South African Veld. It would take a week. So it was a great opportunity for us both to have a little holiday at the BBC's expense. Imagine the cost of that 30-second shot. Three actors, the whole crew and props, probably twelve of us altogether, in an hotel in Marrakech for a week. Then the airfares, and a Moroccan crew, with horses, two were called for but six were there, all for thirty seconds on the screen. I suppose it must have helped, many of the horses and crew we were using were from the enormous set of 'Young Winston' being shot on the other side of the dune, with Simon Ward. The leads in our series were John Halam, who later became successful, and Christopher Casanove, who tragically died of septicaemia recently.

One evening we were invited to a small party given by a crew member. We hadn't been told it was a 'grass' party. Not that I would have known what 'grass' was, other than the obvious skirt. The party congregated in a shabby two roomed flat not far from the hotel. The rooms were filled to overflowing with bleary-eyed, unkempt, slightly smelly people, lolling all over the place.They were on the sofas, the armchairs, leaning against the walls, all very friendly in a spaced-out sort of way. A space on the floor, leaning against a shrinking wall, was made for us and a hand-rolled cigarette passed our way. I've never been able to smoke anything, so I passed it on, I think my wife must have done the same. Then came a simply dreadful glass of Moroccan white wine followed by a plate of very tasty, crisp little biscuits. I took a few, a handful, to disguise the awful taste of the wine. I must say, the biscuits were very nice indeed, I had some more. I said to the unwashed, straggly haired, wan girl leaning against the wall on my right, 'These biscuits are delicious, what's that taste in the background?' She sleepily half laughed, 'They're hash cookies of course.' I half laughed back knowingly, as though the question had been were rhetorical. God, I felt a fool. But they were good, I had another. I was beginning to feel quite merry. Not drunk but merry, happy. I looked at my wife. She didn't look very happy. I said, with a giggle, 'How are you feeling?' She said, 'not like you, obviously.' I giggled. I don't know how long we were there, but on the way back to the hotel I felt I could do anything. I jumped up and walked on the high walls, I spread my arms wide and laughed. 'I can't tell you what a fool you look,' said my wife. I laughed again. At the front desk I asked, in fluent French, how they all were, how were their families, did they have far to go to get back home. 'Can I please have my room key please, thank you, thank you very much indeed, good night, good night, I hope you all sleep well.' I even surprised myself how well I spoke French. I giggled myself to sleep. That was the first and last time I have ever used mind-enhancing drugs, other than antidepressants given to me by a doctor at the Nairobi Hospital, soon after the accident.

Meanwhile, back at the house, our jailbirds were in charge. On our return we could see, straight away, everything 'was shipshape and bristol fashion.' The following morning, I was half the way downstairs, with virtually nothing on, when the older and fatter one opened the front door to come in. He looked up and saw me on the way down, and he said, 'My goodness me sir, you do have beautiful legs sir.' So ironical, if you could see my legs now, thin sticks of bone, smeared with white, sickly, old, parchment-like semblance of skin.

I wonder how they fared. I wonder if they ever achieved any of their dreams. A more pleasant a pair of criminals you could never hope to meet.

***

It's getting closer and closer to the disaster. We said goodbye to my Uncle and Aunt at Gatwick airport in June 1973. We only had three more years of freedom.

If the accident that caused me to be writing my life's story, were bound to happen, you'd have to believe in fate, which I don't think I do. However, the indelible picture of my wife kissing my Aunt Carmen goodbye, with large dewdrop tears suddenly welling up and rolling down her cheeks, must be the first moment that created a chain of circumstances that eventually led to my accident.

My Uncle and Aunt were devoted to one another, so it's especially cruel my aunt had to die of Alzheimer's disease, with all the awful, hurtful symptoms its progress goes through to meet its inevitable, devastating conclusion. My Uncle never wavered, he was by her side until the moment of her death. He rang us from her bedside and said, 'Carmen has just died.' I said, 'Oh Peter, I'm so sorry.' Some of the people he told would say, as words of comfort, 'I'm so sorry, but it was for the best.' On hearing them say those words, he would put those people out of his life. He told me he would cherish any extra moment he could have with her. My wife arranged her funeral to the minutest detail. Every flower had a significant meaning to my Uncle. It was beautiful. To this day, the book of remembrance is open every year, on the date of her death, now with my Uncle's name beside hers, and his ashes, with hers.

Passion for Kenya

Another great friend was given the task of expanding the passion fruit juice industry throughout Kenya, from small holdings to large holdings. A modern juice extraction plant was built, at enormous expense, by a Swiss investment company. It was an excellent idea. Passion fruit is a delicious fruit. It grows quite prolifically in a wide range of climates.

Kenya and the whole of East Africa, Uganda and Tanzania. Right down through Mozambique, Malawi and Botswana, Zimbabwe and into South Africa; could produce enough food, of all description, to feed the world with their range of climates, if organised properly. But to give Africans with very meagre holdings enough incentive to grow a cash crop, rather than subsistence farming is difficult, and to change an understandable mindset even more so. They must be given individual attention so their welfare becomes your responsibility – a big job and long-term investment.

So growing a passion fruit plantation, seemed to us, to be a very pleasant occupation in which to take part. The size of the financial reward depended entirely on the size of the financial input, as with anything. With any farming venture, there is always the added, dreaded factor, of the unknown and the least expected. My father never wanted me to be a farmer of any description. He'd been a farmer all his working life and he maintained farming was littered with disaster, destitution and bankruptcy. He'd lived through the Great Depression, and the first farm he owned had been abandoned by its previous owners. Nevertheless, with the exuberance of youth, it seemed to us, the way of life it offered was far better than living in London with no money.

My father gave us all the land we needed, the river gave us the water, and our house in Clapham and a bank in Nairobi gave us the finance. There were three markets for the fruit. The biggest and the best looking were packed into little boxes surrounded by tissue paper and sent to Europe by aeroplane. They were in the supermarkets all over Europe, at the same time as being consumed by the residents of Nairobi, who were the second market. The third, and possibly the most important, because it underpinned the whole venture, was the pressing of the fruit for their juice. No waste. What could be better?

It took a year to set it all up and to build ourselves a little wooden house near to the plantation. The wooden house was prefabricated by the sawmills our great friend Gwynne's father owned in the forest directly above us in the Highlands. Each prefabricated piece was 7ft high x 10ft long, with door or window spaces as you wished; it was possible to build a house, or room, as big or small as you liked. To make it look as though it was not prefabricated, my wife and my mother thought of turning the whole thing inside out. Then we nailed bark planks, which had been cut off the trunks in the first place, to the outside. It looked as though it had grown up out of the land.

Years before, between the two wars, there'd been a European house built nearby, and in their garden were planted a little group of five jacaranda trees. Here we were, more than fifty years later, doing exactly the same thing, starting from scratch. Those jacaranda trees were beautiful, they glowed a deep, blue-purple in the evening light, and a soft, mellow, inviting shade all through the harsh, heat of a dry African day. They represented to us, a symbol, a beacon of hope and continuity. As it turned out, they were a bright, bright flashing beacon, not of hope and continuity, but of doom and disaster.

***

During that year, we lived in a wing of my parent's home, which was exactly where I was brought up all those years ago. I had come home. Not only in the sense of where I lived as a child, and brought up through adolescence, but a spiritual home, somewhere

I belonged, a profound sensation of satisfaction, being contented with myself. I don't remember ever discussing our situation with my wife. I never asked her if she was happy, if she was happy with the same things that made me feel so contented. I don't think anyone would have done so. Only your behaviour would signify how you felt. We both loved dogs; we had an assortment of five of the most adorable four-legged friends imaginable. Whenever I drove the five minute drive to the plantation, they'd never asked if they could come. They'd fling themselves into the back of my open one-ton truck, all eagerly looking forward over the sides, long pink tongues hanging out, tails wagging. Then, without fail, at the end of the short avenue of old pepper trees, planted by the same people who'd planted the group of five jacaranda trees, they'd hurl themselves out of the moving truck. They'd dash in front, leading the way down yet another drive, built by the same people, to the plantation. Quite often, while dashing along, one of them would pick-up a thorn in their pad. He or she would come grinding to a halt, pick up their paw and look back at me, tongue falling to one side. I'd have to stop the truck, get out, kneel down, all the others shoving their wet noses in my face, take out the thorn. I'd rub the pad better, as Ahdiga did for me, and they'd all charge off before I'd had a chance of getting back in the truck.

During the fruiting season, three times a week, I'd take a ton of fruit, packed in little boxes with tissue paper, to the shipping agents in Nairobi. They'd take the load, with many others, to the airport. I'd also make other journeys into Nairobi with full sacks, to the fruit market, to the grocers around the city, and to the juice factory. Often, after the deliveries, we'd go to the cinema, then to one of the many excellent restaurants. Sometimes we'd drop in on our great friends, Peter and Jo in Karen, or to Gwynne, in Limuru. Limuru stood at 7500 feet so we often drove through deep fog and darkness on the way back to our little wooden house on the floor of the Great Rift Valley. Then the greeting ceremony, with our joyful, laughing, four-legged army of the most faithful friends, all dog owners would know about.

On the way in to make my deliveries I'd always pass the main house, where my parents lived, say hello and drop off whatever fruit they needed. It was after one of these occasions, My mother told me later, she'd said to my father, 'Surely you must agree he's doing well now.' He said, 'Yes, but I've seen it all before, something unexpected will come along, and knock him for six.' Oh Dear, Oh Dear, how right he was. In a few weeks time, not only would I be knocked for six, I'd be knocked out of the game entirely.

We'd lived exactly a year in our little house, and apart from my childhood up to the age of nine, I've described earlier, that was the best year I can remember I'd ever lived. I can't speak for my wife because I now know she never wanted to leave England in the first place. That indelible picture, that clear crisp snapshot of shining round, rolling tears, welling up in her dark-brown eyes, and flowing down her cheeks, when saying goodbye to my Aunt at Gatwick Airport, will always remain with me till the day I die. What was about to happen would knock most people off course forever.

***

The first event, however, was not the car crash. The car crash was a calamity of its own... what was about to happen, would set it up.

We were late back home, our usual evening out, and on opening the front door, a sea of jumping, smiling, laughing, licking, pink-tongued dogs confronted us. My mother's four, as well as our own. In the middle of the sitting room was a mound of the most extraordinary collection of things; clocks, silver teapots, cutlery, copper-ware, ornaments, a mad burglar's hoard, bundled-up in a carpet. Our cook-house-man suddenly appeared, looking fraught and worried. He said in Swahili, 'Your parents had to leave their house, your lorry is full of their things and they're staying at the club in Nairobi.' There was so much to ask him, but he couldn't articulate what was going on. It was obviously too late to go to the club now, we'd go first thing in the morning.

They were in the dining room, peacefully having breakfast together. My father, reading the newspaper, my mother mixing her honey with the butter, as she always did, before covering a torn-off corner of toast. My father said, 'Oh hello Mennit, what are you doing here?' I just looked at him, jaw hanging. He went on, 'We've been chucked out, I'll ring Gichuru, next thing.' James

Gichuru and he got on really quite well. I'm not sure why, or what had brought them together in the first place, but James Gichuru had been the Minister for Defence in Jomo Kenyatta's first cabinet. Most unfortunately, he'd fallen for the lure of that delicious amber liquid, usually distilled in Scotland. Although no longer actively a Minister, he was still well respected, but any business, other than chit-chat, had to be conducted before 11 o'clock in the morning.

The whole issue of land ownership, in all newly independent countries in Africa, is a very sensitive area for anyone to tread, even if you'd owned land legally for years. Jomo Kenyatta, before he became president, and the British Government both realised, the change from European to African ownership must happen quite quickly but in an orderly fashion. The British Government would compensate farmers for agricultural land but not for cattle ranching. Ranching was much less sensitive an area as most of the tribes, primarily, wanted their agricultural land, and 'The White Highlands' in particular, given back to them. The Europeans had taken it from them, as they saw it, and they wanted it back. They weren't going to pay anything for it, it was theirs. If the British Government wanted to pay something to the British farmers, then that was up to them. All the agricultural land had good regular rainfall and was fertile. The ranching land, the plains, had no permanent source of water. Nobody then, other than perceptive, imaginative and entrepreneurial Europeans, such as my father, could make any use out of it.

So that's how my father still had his land. He'd brought water to it from a long way away. No one but him would have thought of bringing water to his ranch from the source he did. Water is a very precious commodity anywhere in Africa, so to move it from one piece of land to another requires a strictly observed water permit. The Officer arrived to see the source from which the water was to be taken. He just laughed at my father's scheme, and gave him permission there and then. The source was a small swamp of about five acres well within the boundaries of the forestry commission and unused by anyone other than the forest animals and birds. He found it completely by chance; it was his exploratory instinct that took him there.

The very first thing he did was to build a hide for us children to come with him in the evenings to watch the forest animals. Waterbuck, Buffalo, small diker, a profusion of bird life, and even on occasion, although it must have happened every night, a leopard. How exciting it was to be with him. The Cook was told to make sandwiches and little buck steaks, a thermos of tea, and then we'd set off in single file. No talking, as quietly as possible, through the forest, to the flat plateau above, that so unexpectedly contained the small swamp. Then into our beautiful newly constructed, almost invisible, little hide.

All this incredible excitement could only happen three days a month, before, at, and after, full moon. So it was only once in a blue moon, all the conditions were perfect. The water he took from the swamp made no difference to the conditions of the marsh in any way and he was able to water, through a system of enormous round stone tanks, thousands of his cattle all over the ranch. Each herd, of around two hundred head, mustn't graze too close to each watering point, as too many cattle gathering together in any one place creates a dust bowl. All this development required careful management and had been going on ever since I could remember. And yet my brother and I were sent away to school, away from something we loved, away from where we belonged.

***

By this time, the late 1970's, Jomo Kenyatta, was getting old. But being the 'Father of the Nation', replacing him was impossible to contemplate. However, there were rumblings, and sometimes the rumblings were more than just a tremor. He dealt with them ruthlessly. But it was after one of these rumblings, he, Jomo Kenyatta, made a rabble-rousing tour of the whole country. His speeches weren't thought through, they were off-the-cuff, saying whatever the people wanted to hear. Does that sound familiar, about any politician anywhere? Of course it does. I don't think he really meant to use the phraseology that was construed to mean the Europeans should now be forced to relinquish their ranchlands for 50 shillings an acre, less than 50p now, about £2 then, but that's how it came about. My father was approached by a Cooperative based in the town of Limuru, in the heart of Jomo Kenyatta's tribe land, to sell his home ranch to them for £11,500. He hadn't thought about it, let alone approached anybody. As far as they were concerned a refusal wasn't an option. They'd collected the money from all the shareholders and The President said they could have it. The Chairman told all the shareholders he had paid Mr Mayers the money, so they could now occupy the house and farm.

So to return to my parents peacefully having breakfast at the club. My father spoke to James Gichuru before 11 o'clock. 'Disgraceful,' he said with real anger in his voice, 'I'll speak to Charles immediately.' Charles, was Charles Njonjo, The Attorney-General, a very clever and powerful man. But even he found very quickly that he had to tread extremely carefully in this particular case. We had an appointment to see him in just a few days. In his outer office waiting with us, was the entire cooperative committee, dirty clothes, hands in pockets, leaning against the walls, lolling in the armchairs, with an air of insolence. My father and I and our lawyer were called into the main office. The whole committee shuffled in with us and loosely settled themselves in all the available chairs in the same insolent manner. Charles Njonjo came in from his inner office, he looked at them for a moment and said with a voice that could cut-glass, 'Get out.' They straightened up, hands from pockets, momentarily looked awkward, briefly turned to each other, and quickly shuffled out. He looked at my father and said with real feeling, 'I'm very sorry about what has happened.' My father said 'Thank you.' Njongo then said, 'I can get your house back for you, but I'm very sorry to have to say, although it's completely within your right to refuse, if you don't let them have your land,' he paused, looked down, then looked up, and said slowly, 'you could be in great danger.' A long silence followed. He, looking at my father, and my father, looking at him. We all rose together, shook hands and filed out.

We drove back to our lawyer's office to sum up. A small adjustment could be made to their offer. They would have to pay something for the passion fruit plantation and our wooden house. My Parents would retain the main house with its garden and surrounding acres, but most importantly and urgently, we needed night and day security to establish our ownership of the Family House.

While all this was going on, my mother, my sister-in-law and her two children, had disappeared off to the coast, to stay with my Aunt Ginger. In view of what Njonjo had warned, my father wanted my wife to go too, but she refused. The house was vacated without any damage, so when everything from our little house and the back of my lorry was put back in place, it didn't look as though anything had happened at all. Our day and night 'Guard' consisted of twelve men in uniform with rifles, and a Sergeant. Our Sergeant was the smartest Sergeant you've ever seen. His uniform was dark air-force blue, with razor-sharp creases down the front of his trousers, his gaiters and belt shining white. The buckles and badge of gleaming brass, the toes of his boots, such a bright, deep black, they caught the sun as he marched about, barking orders to his men. This little pantomime went on for about a week. I don't know if it served any purpose, but at least we were safe. My wife and I drove down to the valley floor, from the main house to the plantation, to pay wages to all the workers, for the last time. In the same way we'd made a pitch to show our ownership of the big house, I suppose they did the same to show their ownership of the plantation and the rest of my father's land. During the payout, a swarm of screaming, yelling young men descended upon us, tearing open the neat boxes of fruit and ripping open the sacks, ready for the Nairobi deliveries. They wildly crammed whole fruit into their mouths so the juice and seeds spurted out over their faces. The workers were terrified, they didn't know whether to run away or stay for their last weekly wage. Without a word between us, we acted as though nothing was amiss. Our headman's heart was pumping so hard you could see it heaving through his chest. I gave him the money for each person, and he handed it out. He was very brave to stay. It seemed to take an age to finish. I locked the door of the store in which I was standing to do the payout, and they immediately smashed it open. We climbed back into the truck, with all the screaming shouting young men, waving their pangas (long knives) in the air, and slowly drove away.

I started this agonising tale with what was going to happen in about two months time. You can see clearly now how the sequence of events came about. To be waiting for the butcher on that beautiful day, on the 29th of June 1976, to drive north through the little ramshackle, wooden town of Rumeruti and the beginning of years of traumatic despair.

In the time-honoured phrase, 'life goes on', it does go on, but it so often does so in a manner that's cruel beyond measure. About 18 months after the car crash, my little wife and I were well ensconced with our marvellous new friend Marriott, in her small mews house in Notting Hill Gate, West London. One evening, after her usual delicious, simple supper and a bottle or two of red wine, the telephone rang. I picked up the receiver, there was a long echoing silence, a feeling of dread came over me. A soft, distant, fragile, small voice said, 'Hello Darling, Daddy's had a stroke, he's in Nairobi hospital.' I weep when I remember that far away, fragile, soft little voice. Somehow, we were there, at my father's bedside, the next day. The stroke could not have been crueler to a man like my father. A man with such life and vitality, such humour, everyone remembers his laugh, such gentleness, such strength, so many ideas, so full of thought, everything taken away. He couldn't speak, not even a murmur, he couldn't think, he couldn't feed himself. He couldn't walk, he had no coordination, he couldn't even control his bowels and bladder. And yet, with his whole character taken away, he was left with his physical life, and the ability to feel terrible, agonising, contorting pain. We didn't know then, but I'm pretty certain I know now, after 18 exhausting, emotionally draining months for my poor mother, he died in such awful, dreadful agony of a massive heart attack. As it was happening, he was trying to tell the doctor, by pointing to the side of his stomach, but actually he was trying to point to his chest. My mother was with him in the Mission Hospital above the Kedong Valley, holding his hand as the last embers of his life faded away and he was finally, still.

The Vineyard

In spite of all we'd been through in our life together, right up until we found ourselves looking out from our 'ivory tower' on to the moving picture of activity on the River Thames just east of Tower Bridge; we still had no direction of how or where our life might lead. I was still drowning in my own, my own dreadful dissatisfaction and lack of purpose and uselessness of my life, and I was beginning to pull my poor little wife down with me.

A local social worker came to see us and welcome us into the area. What were our plans and could he be involved in any way? It turned out he strongly disapproved of all the warehouses along the banks of the river being turned into expensive housing, forcing the local population back and back, from what they considered 'their' river. They were being forced into poorer and poorer, run down accommodation that hadn't really featured in any government planning since the end of the Second World War. He hated Margaret Thatcher with a vengeance, but it was her policies that incentivised inner-city development throughout the country. One of her aims was to move wealth from the generally wealthy South of England, through the Midlands and on to the genuinely deprived north-east; Grimsby, Hull, Darlington and Newcastle. Even today the North-east is lagging behind the South-east, and it's the massively expensive construction of HS2 that's now thought to be the answer to moving wealth north.

There was nothing we could say to appease our social worker, as then, he was right. I wonder what he'd say now. I know it's taken thirty years, but the East End of London, all around the derelict docks and warehouses, is now sought after and thriving.

The whole of the warehouse building plan could not have turned out better. We'd completed the entire project, selling the two lower floors to pay back bank loans. We still owned the freehold and a double storied penthouse with an outside rooftop garden. We had a lift from our basement garage right up to the top floor, and didn't owe a penny to anyone, not even a mortgage. That's not strictly true. My generous mother had written-off her loan, saying it would come out of my inheritance. I didn't deserve such kindness. What we didn't know was its success was to be pivotal in pointing us in the direction our lives would take for the next forty years.

Living on the bank of this mighty river, flowing through the centre of one of the greatest cities in the world, was a thrilling experience. Floating past our balcony was all manner of craft, from warships to pleasure boats, from tall-ships to ocean-going sailing ships. There were tough little tugs, pulling teams of barges laden to the gunnels with all types of goods. Some were destined for the massive cargo ships docked at Tilbury, others filled with London's rubbish, to be dumped in the Estuary for the high tides to take to the North Sea and beyond.

We had all this, but we still had no income or direction in our lives. The reality was stark. For the previous five years we'd been living with our miraculous Marriott, who'd looked after us with her enveloping warmth and gentle care. Now suddenly, here we were, completely alone. My poor little wife felt desperately lonely. She was only thirty-five, in the prime of her life, staring into a dreadful trap of nothing but me to look after, with me drinking too much, for the foreseeable future. I understood her despair, but I couldn't see what I could do about it, other than stop drinking.

I've told you about our beautiful, small, strong-willed four-legged wonder. It's their devotion to each other that was such a comfort to my little wife. I don't really know if dogs do know if there's anything wrong with the people who love them, but it is possible to read that devotion into a 'knowing', when there is unhappiness.

My Uncle and Aunt had also become incredibly fond and in love, they would say, of our little wonder. We were beginning to think we should the use the escalating value of the warehouse, to buy a little house in the country to broaden our horizon. They used any excuse to be as close to us as possible, so they started looking around them in East Sussex, for something suitable. My Uncle had been a major in the Cameron Highlanders. One of his wartime jobs was to set up an extremely secretive system of Operational Bases (OBs) from east to west along the Scottish border in 1942, when the possibility of invasion of Britain seemed imminent. Peter had a talent for finding opportunities in any given situation. In no time at all we had a summons. A derelict barn, not a mile away from them, set in its own parcel of south-facing twenty acres of land to be sold by sealed tender on the 15th of September 1984. Sealed tender is a Scottish method of selling property. All interested parties must place their bids by post, to be opened at the specified time and date. The highest bid wins. It's very difficult to decide upon a price, if you don't know what price to bid against. To try the system out, we placed our own bids in a hat to test if any of us knew what the value might be. Only between the four of us, the bids varied from £48,000 to £145,000! How on earth were we to decide? After a great deal of discussion, lasting days on end, we came to an agreement at £ 51,500! To this day, we have no idea by how much we won, or if indeed, we were the only bid! However, its acquisition sealed our future.

One of the best days of our lives was the day we planted our vineyard but after fifteen exhausting, anxious years, came the second-best day of our lives. We pulled it out! But before that final day, by a set of peculiar circumstances, a woman who I'll call Cathy, came into our lives. She would undertake all the manual work I would have undertaken had I not been paraplegic. She worked like a Trojan. She did everything. She drove the tractor. She changed all the various pieces of equipment necessary to keep the vines free of weeds and grasses. She trained all the 6000 vines to their wires. She kept them all pruned and sprayed, against all manner of fungi and diseases. She started early and she worked late. And she loved her work. She was 'Wonder Woman'. I'd fallen on my feet!

I can't remember why or how I started to become allergic to her character. I'm embarrassed at my behaviour towards somebody whose sole purpose was to work for me with all of her ability. She'd found a job for which she was prepared to give everything, her whole self. I don't think of myself as a cruel person but, I'm ashamed to say, I was cruel to poor Cathy.

I don't know if it was because of me she started drinking or because of her dreadful family life. We weren't aware of when it started, but in retrospect we should have put two and two together. On one occasion we'd been away for a few days, so Cathy looked after the house. On our return, under all the cushions on the sofas in the kitchen, not well hidden, we discovered empty bottle after empty bottle of cider. It still didn't occur to us she had a problem.

Around the back of the house, we'd given her a two-bed caravan as she wanted to be quiet and alone. It had a cooker, so she could make herself a cup of tea or coffee and be nice and warm for her lunch in the winter. I'd noted she wasn't around the vineyard as much as perhaps she should have been, and I'd find her sound asleep on one of the beds in the caravan. And even though a rather unpleasant, pungent odour seemed to follow her about, it still didn't register on either of us that she'd become an alcoholic.

Finally, finally late one night, perhaps after an incident at home, she decided to drive to work and poor Cathy smashed her car into the rear of a stationary vehicle in the village. The police arrived upon the scene. Fortunately, she wasn't hurt, but she was found wandering around the village dragging a piece of the car into which she'd just collided. Poor woman, she was five times over the limit.

She asked me to be a character witness at her trial. I owed her that at least. But she lost her licence for a couple of years. To add to her misery, I had to tell her, 'Surely, Cathy you can't go on coming to work without a car.' She said, 'I know you want to get rid of me, but I'm not going, this is my job.'

She did stay, walking the seven miles from her house every morning. She was never late, but soon, it became untenable and she became quite ill. She died in the cottage hospital from drink-related complications.

Over the first ten years we were here and before the tragic drama of Cathy's downfall and eventual demise, we'd had to sell the warehouse, convert the derelict barn, and establish a whole new way of life.

The first blow was the refusal of planning permission by the Wealden District Council. We had been warned by our solicitor that this would happen, but by law we could take the decision to appeal. On the town council were twelve members of the public, and apparently it was quite legitimate to lobby each member separately. They all responded in the affirmative to our argument, except one who said she would listen to the pros and cons put forward by the council officers on the day.

Our argument was we were saving a beautiful old Sussex barn, first erected in the seventeenth century, from dereliction. Now that a vineyard had been established, it was necessary for the manager or owner to live on-site. On the other hand the Council officers argued, it wasn't worth saving as it was so remote, no members of the public would ever see it. Also, there were many other, far better preserved examples, all over the county. Also all services necessary for a modern dwelling, water, electricity, waste collection, sewage and bins would be difficult and expensive for the council to implement. A reasonable argument, but our lobbying, fortunately, paid off. Every single member, even the woman who said she'd decide on the day, voted for us.

Gavin, the builder we used, is still a very good friend to this day. He told us that anything he built he'd give it a lifetime guarantee! He's always kept an eye on us and regularly drops in for a chat. Every year we get a bottle of champagne on each of our birthdays and one for Christmas. He told us he'd take a year to build the house as it was a difficult and complicated conversion. He moved his team on-site on November 21st. 1985. On November the 21st 1986, all was completed. The underfloor heating made the house as warm as toast; a welcome bottle of champagne awaited us in the fridge. We moved in!

In October 1987 it was now evident poor Cathy had worked superbly in the vineyard, so our first crop was ready for picking. It would be small, but nevertheless a very exciting and rewarding achievement.

I've told you earlier my father never wanted me to have anything to do with farming. 'The risks are too high for a viable long-term future. I've seen too many farmers completely ruined overnight.' What did he mean exactly?

On the morning of October the 18th 1987, I found myself on the telephone, speaking to my wife, who was staying with her brother in Herefordshire, saying, 'We are ruined.' I now knew what my father meant. Everyone in the South-east of England had woken up to the results of the most devastating storm, with hurricane winds, usually associated with the tropics. All the vines were stripped off the wires, lying flat on the ground. All Cathy's long, hard, tedious work over the previous three years, gone to nothing in only a few hours. My mother was staying with me, and she came padding through to my room at about three in the morning and said, 'Is this normal for Sussex?' For the last 55 years she'd lived in Kenya, in very remote places, even when my father was away in North Africa in 1943 fighting the war. She'd been confronted with an enormous variety of life-threatening dangers, but she'd never been in a storm like this.

The only option open was to start again. It was ten years since that car spun out of control, rolling over and over and my back snapped, cutting the spinal cord, leaving me paralysed from the waist down. Only now had I come to terms with my disability and realised my only option was to 'start again'.

Poor Cathy took it in her stride, beginning at one end of the vineyard and not stopping until the job was done. All the family were procured whenever they could see a spare moment. My mother, my little sister, Peter and Carmen, C's Brothers and their wives, women from the village, other passers-by, anyone, and everyone was collared. They were given a ball of string and scissors and sent out into the vineyard to twist and tie the fallen vines back on the wire.

We'd lost our first crop but the second benefited, and with renewed vigour, which soon started to show. From then on the tonnage produced grew and grew. One particularly good year, the setting in May wasn't hit by frost or rain. It was a lovely hot long summer and the rainfall was perfect; not too hard, not too much and not too little. The autumn was soft and warm, perfect for happy pickers; the best were young mums from the village who had to leave at three to collect their little darlings from school. On that year, we produced thirty tons of utterly delectable, sweet, full-bodied, disease free, bunches of grapes. That perfect combination of weather conditions only comes about, on average, once every ten or twelve years. In the intervening years the romanticism of producing your own wine, turns to pulling your hair out with worry and frustration.

Luckily for us, the large vineyard nearby, Lamberhurst Vineyard, owned then by the McAlpine Family, awarded us a very generous contract to take all our grapes for the next few years. Thank you, Mr. McAlpine.

Breaking down

Slowly, almost imperceptibly, the health and fitness of our 'oldies', my mother, Peter and Carmen, inevitably started to break-down. Carmen, who was the brightest, quickest, wittiest of people began to show signs of some sort of character change. Peter couldn't put his finger on it. An X-ray revealed an enormous tumour, the size of a golf ball in the centre of her brain between the two halves, not attached and very fortunately, not malignant. With careful surgery, it could be removed. The Maudsley Hospital in London performed the delicate operation. However, although she recovered well, Peter said it was from then her personality slowly began to subtly alter. In only about three years Peter, with awful remorseful regret, was forced to conclude he could no longer look after her. He felt he was letting her down, letting himself down, letting down the sixty years of happiness and devotion they had for one another. To put her into a 'home' specialising in the cruellest of illness, Alzheimer's disease, was heartbreaking. He was by her side every day, even when she didn't know him, for two years until she died.

After my father's catastrophic, debilitating stroke, my brother made arrangements to leave South Africa, where he was living with his family, and move back to the farm in the Kedong Valley to help my mother with its running. He moved into a little cottage on the other side of the river with only one bedroom. This cottage was generally reserved for a manager or was let to weekenders from Nairobi. So for him to squeeze his whole family into this little house, while my mother rattled around in the main house, was hardly conducive to a satisfactory relationship.

There are often two sides to most family conflicts, so my poor mother could well have been the architect of her own unhappiness. In her life with my father, she'd often taken the initiative when he'd boxed himself into an unsolvable problem, and found the way out. I, as a child and teenager, had often presented her with a predicament of my own, knowing she'd have the answer. So now, to be part of the problem, why didn't she take the initiative and clear a way through?

The answer was as plain as day; she had to give in, and swap houses. But my brother refused to make the changes she wanted to the house in which he was living, so, in turn she refused to move out of her house. My brother's obstinacy matched her own. As a consequence, it was ten years of unnecessary deterioration to the relationship between him and my mother. She then became too frail to go back and forth from England to Kenya, and he finally moved into her house which he always assumed was his inheritance anyway.

My little wife began to feel crowded in upon. Between the five of us, my mother, Peter and Carmen and ourselves, she was the only able-bodied person. We all relied on her. She couldn't get away. She had no space of her own. It was during one of these episodes of oppression, she spotted an obscure, two lined advert on the property page in the Daily Telegraph. It described a charming little one bedroom cottage, hidden away on its own land in the hills overlooking the sea near Brindisi, Puglia, Southern Italy. She had to see it there and then. This was the answer. She immediately rang the agent in Puglia. 'I must see it tomorrow, how do I get there?' I couldn't deflect her. Literally, the following day, we were on a Ryan Air flight, costing one pound each, from Stanstead Airport to Brindisi in Southern Italy.

We were met at the airport by an Irishman called Justin. This meeting turned out to be the beginning of a five-year building project that still goes on to this day, ten years later.

The whole scheme emphasises if you want to go abroad for a holiday, stay in a hotel. Stay in a hotel for as long as you like, wherever you like. Stay in a five-star hotel, eat whatever you like, drink the best wines on offer every night. It will still be cheaper than owning your own house in a foreign country. If anything goes wrong, ring reception and it'll be put right. If you step out of your room, by the time you get back, all the towels will be changed, the bed made up, the soaps changed, the bathroom sparkling and the minibar filled. If you don't like staying in a hotel and you want to do everything yourself, rent a house. Rent whatever house you like, with a cook or without a cook, but whatever you do, please, please don't buy a house abroad!

The advertisement was quite right, it was a charming little casa with views over the sea, standing in its own grounds. It had olive trees, almond trees, fig trees, pine trees – it was lovely. It had steps up to a flat roof for evening drinks. It was just as you'd imagine a perfect little cottage should be in Southern Italy. I couldn't actually get into it. All the windows were too high for me to see out of. You had to buy water by the bowser-full. I couldn't climb up to the flat roof for quiet evening drinks, but who was I to complain about such trivialities. We built our little house in Kenya in the middle of nowhere, without any services whatsoever. My little wife needed a break, she had to have somewhere to get away, be on her own, away from all the pressure crowding in. We bought it and everything was made accessible for me.

What we didn't know at the time was, in Italy there are two prices for all agricultural properties. The first is an agricultural value and the second is a market value. The agricultural value is the sum stated as its real value at the time of purchase. The sum on which you pay all relevant taxes, stamp duty, commune duties, etc. is paid to the vendor, in front of the Notary and it's signed and sealed then and there. At that moment, the property legally changes hands and becomes the property of the purchaser. The agreed sum is then seen to be given to the vendor by the buyer. There is also an English-speaking translator, in our case a girl from Birmingham, explaining all procedure as you go along. The Notary then stands, shakes everyone by the hand, and says in Italian, translated by the girl from Birmingham, 'I just have to go outside for a few minutes; I believe you have a little business to discuss.'

Our agent, sitting at the back of the room, clutching our Banker's Drafts, moved centre stage and formally handed the remainder to the vendor with a little bow. The vendor graciously accepted them likewise.

A part of the service our agent offered was to oversee all the building work on the properties they sold. I suspect they made that promise not realising how successful their business was about to become. At one stage I believe they were closing one sale every day of the week and each sale required an awful amount of work. Each transaction was, more than likely, to be one of the more important events in any purchaser's life.

Justin's agency consisted of himself and a brilliant, beautiful Armenian girl called Anna. If we were an example of any one of their clients, there weren't enough hours in a day for them to deal with all our ever increasing expectations. Over the next five years the number of emails I sent Anna, and expected an immediate response, would have filled a library. When their involvement was finally over, I wrote her an email. I said how much we appreciated all the time and effort they'd put in, on our behalf and, 'I'm going to miss our little chats.' She wrote back, 'I wouldn't call them "little chats", I'd call them Small Talks.'

We never did get our hideaway used for its original intention. By the time it was finished all our oldies had departed, "flown to others we know not of". First, poor Carmen, then it was the turn of my poor mother to start to fade. She shouldn't have been here, in this country. She should have been in my brother's house in the Kedong Valley. But she was well looked after, sustained financially by those shares my brother-in-law bought for her, all those years ago when I was on that Stryker bed in Nairobi hospital.

She'd always been an avid reader, so one of the jobs was to supply her with at least seven books a week. But that appetite slowly started to decline, and television took over. In its turn the interest in television waned and she would just sit staring ahead, agitated, troubled, waiting for someone to come and sit with her. One afternoon we were both with her and she said, 'Dr Davis came to see me this morning.' We knew he was monitoring her so it wasn't surprising. So I said, 'That was kind of him, what did he have to say.' She said, 'That's the curious thing, he didn't say anything. He came in through the window, walked straight past me, and went out through the door.' I said, 'I must admit that is a strange thing to do, especially as your window is on the first floor.' She said, 'I'm glad you agree with me, I thought I was seeing things.'

She had another episode of seeing a pretty little girl, dressed in a white party dress with a blue satin ribbon tied around her waist. She was dancing about the room while one of the staff was making up her bed. The little girl disappeared into her cupboard just as the member of staff was about to leave the room. It turned out she was harbouring a respiratory infection and Dr. Davis really did have to make a visit, this time through her door.

She rallied after a short course of antibiotics and realised what had happened. She said, with a whimsical smile, 'I do miss my little girl though.'

It is strange how, sometimes, wonderful things do happen at the very worst of times. As I know only too well. One of the other inmate's daughter, would visit her mother most days and occasionally meet my mother around the house. They slowly found they were looking forward to seeing each other, so they arranged to have tea together once a week. This quickly turned into twice a week. Judith became a very close friend. My mother's whole attitude changed. She'd unwittingly let herself fall into the depths of despair. She just wanted it all to be over. Then quite suddenly, up popped Judith. Her attitude changed. Rather than just sitting in her room staring at the wall, expressionless, waiting for someone to come in, she would get dressed, put on her trainers and pad about the house visiting others in their rooms. Judith and her husband Geoffrey, a number of times, asked her out for lunch to their intriguing farmhouse nearby. Geoffrey farmed beef cattle and occasionally he would cull a deer. He and Judith would prepare the whole animal for the freezer. This was an entire day's work for two people. How could my mother ever have known, all these years later in England, she would be watching exactly the same preparation of an animal she had undertaken herself, after she had killed a Thompson's gazelle when she first came to Kenya in 1937.

A glimpse of her former self, began to emerge. Since having to leave the Kedong Valley she'd become a depleted person, she became small and frail. In her prime, during all my formative years, she was a tall, strong, broad-shouldered woman able to take on anything.

I can picture her so well, when my father was away for weeks on end buying cattle in the northern frontier of Kenya. She and our Headman Marratim, he standing just outside the veranda on the lawn, and my mother at her table in the shade, updating a huge ledger, containing the health and well-being of all the cattle on the farm. Marratim spoke in a mellifluous, descriptive mix of Swahili and his own dialect, Nandi, and painted her a picture of the state of each animal in every herd. At any one time she could tell my father how many head were ready for slaughter, how many were not very well or underweight. Also, how many were calving and how many needed intensive care and feeding in the boma on the other side of the river from the main house.

She always had a project going on in the garden, expanding, improving. If she needed more labour for any expansion project, both Di Di and Marratim would vet anyone before they could be employed.

All these images came flooding back to her. Instead of being saddened, comparing them to herself in her present situation, I think she could look back with pleasure at all she had achieved. Now my brother was able to take advantage of all her extensive endeavours.

Although her frame had shrunk and her little shoulders were bent, a faint glint in her eyes brightened her face and she had the air of being so much more at peace with herself.

It wasn't long before the cruel shroud of insidious old age settled over her and she could no longer leave her room. Nevertheless two afternoons every week, without fail, Judith was with her to lighten her day. Thank you, Judith.

When we were told by the excellent staff the end was close, we stayed on after her supper, consisting only of a few small sips of light warm broth through a straw. My wife gently held her small soft reduced hand, which every now and then gave a tiny squeeze of acknowledgement, until we fell asleep in our chairs. The night staff kindly found us a single bed in which we could gratefully curl together, and they said they would call us when the time came. Morning broke and her chest was still quietly, almost imperceptibly, rising and falling. So we went home to freshen up to come straight back.

One of the nurses looking after her was a tall, kind robust girl with a very gentle manner. The bed had been heightened to enable everyone tending her not to have to bend down, when changing sheets for example. The sheets needed changing. The tall, strong nurse carefully slipped her arms underneath my mother's little reduced body and held her in her arms, while two others quickly renewed the sheets. While my mother was in her arms, she died. We arrived back five minutes later.

My little wife arranged a beautiful goodbye service, with all the flowers my mother loved the most, on a wicker coffin. I wrote the eulogy which my wife read out. We sent her ashes to my Brother in the Kedong Valley and he arranged another small service for the few close family still living there, and buried her ashes next to my father's coffin.

Uncle Peter

Uncle Peter was now the last of our responsibilities. He was ninety, but a remarkable ninety-year-old. His mind was still as sharp as ever and his sense of humour just as 'wicked'. Ever since he left the army, at forty-six he pursued his two great interests as part of his working life, skiing and tennis.

I don't think there was any country in the world he and Carmen hadn't visited. They did it their business to know, in detail, how every country worked and its place in history, its place on the map. Their minds were as sharp as each others and their sense of humour fitted as smoothly as perfectly timed machines. They were both outstandingly good-looking and unusually charming, so everywhere they went they made wonderful company. Carmen could speak every European language as fluently as her own tongue. They would seem to be a couple with everything and they knew that was how they came across. Instead of being pleased with themselves they were amused by the effect they had on others and they made many very good friends.

It was they who toured around England visiting school after school, deciding which one they felt would be the most suitable for me. Without meaning to misrepresent me, they gave all the schools a far greater expectation of my abilities than I could possibly deliver.

Innocently, unknowingly I arrived at their final choice of school, armed with a sports scholarship and an enviable ability in all subjects in the classroom! The reality could not have been further from the truth. I couldn't be bothered to try to be good at anything, whether in the classroom or on the playing field. I was the archetypal lazy, useless schoolboy doing only just enough to get by.

It wasn't financially viable to go home to Kenya more than once a year, so I tagged along with Peter and Carmen most of the time. When I told them how disappointing I seemed to be to the school, instead of taking it seriously and perhaps giving me some advice, they treated it as a huge source of amusement.

I suppose this is how it's meant to work, the older generation look after the younger, then, in turn the younger look after the older. So here we were with Peter at ninety. He died suddenly three years later. I can honestly say there wasn't a single day it wasn't a pleasure to be with him. One day he drove down the hill from his cottage to the vineyard as usual, not looking very well, sallow. He flopped himself on to the sofa in the kitchen and said, 'I'm feeling awful, I haven't slept a wink all night.' We were naturally concerned. He went on, 'I've got too much money.' This piece of information was quite a relief, but surprising in its delivery. He and Carmen were renowned for being very careful with their money, to say the least. 'I could have done so much more for Carmen.' He'd got that the wrong way round, it was Carmen who did the saving. All her life she'd set herself the task to doing everything for less money than anyone else. Whenever we stopped for the night on one of our many trips, she'd say to Peter and me, 'How much do you think I can get off the cost of the room?' She'd win every time. She prided herself the only cheque she'd ever written was when she bought herself a mink coat just before the war.

Now, Peter was to 'set-about' spending as much money he could before he died. He took us on our first ever cruise in the Mediterranean Sea. He bought us a new car so we could drive him for a wonderful trip to his beloved Switzerland, to be on the snow one more time before he died. He enjoyed it so much we did it again. He liked to organise everything to the last detail. He had a phenomenal memory. He loved to find places, the exact place he'd stood with Carmen on any one of hundreds of times he'd been skiing with her over the sixty years they'd been married. They'd always found each other amusing, so when we'd found an exact place, he'd chuckle at the memory of what Carmen had done or said. He'd never spent money so easily before, and he found it a liberating experience. Mind you, if he had spent money in the way he was doing at this point, he wouldn't have it to spend now, Catch-22. He liked to be with us whenever we drove anywhere. On one occasion, we had to go to the funeral of a relative of my wife. He came along, stayed in the car with his newspaper while we were in the church, then we drove back home.

Another very successful thing he invested in, which he'd never have dreamt of doing before this new-found liberation was 'Sky Sport'. I told you earlier, his other abiding interest was tennis. He'd follow all the top players, men and women, all around the world. He knew everything about each player. Not just their game, their lives off court as well. He liked to be alone in his cottage in the evenings. He'd pour himself two large whiskeys and cook himself his supper. Always the same, a fillet of grilled salmon reluctantly accompanied with boiled broccoli because it was good for him. One of the things he did after leaving the army was to be the Secretary of the Ski Club of Great Britain, Eaton Square in London. He was there for twelve years. Of course part of the job then was to go to Switzerland and Austria and France for three months of the year, to represent the Club and help members with whatever problems they might have. The remaining nine months he worked at the club itself. He wrote a book covering and rating every single ski resort in Switzerland, Austria and France by skiing and staying the night in every one.

I've told you how much he liked to organise. The Club suddenly found it started to make money. Not by putting up subscriptions or cutting down on staff, purely organisation. The Club ran an excellent little restaurant for members and one of the items on the menu was steak and kidney pie. Peter had his table reserved for lunch and every day, for nine months of the year, for twelve years he had steak and kidney pie.

Every Sunday he came to the vineyard for lunch, and of course I cooked him the same thing each time. Crispy streaky bacon with very thin slices of lamb's liver. He didn't like vegetables so we let him off as it was Sunday.

One Sunday he came in holding a large cardboard box under his arm. He said, 'Read through all the files so you know where everything is, and you can get them to the solicitor quickly after I die.' We knew he'd left everything to us because he'd brought his solicitor here to draw up his will. He excluded all other members of the family and left us his house and all his money. But we didn't know how much money or where it was. When I did see how much money was coming our way, my Good little wife insisted he must include my two sisters and my brother. He reluctantly agreed, but wouldn't write it in the will itself, because he couldn't work out how much we'd have to pay in death duties. The value of the cottage would be added to the whole estate that would be taxed, and could vary significantly. So he said, 'Only give away what think you can afford. It was a good thing for the others my wife was the executor. If it was left up to me, it's unlikely I would have been able to afford to give the others as much as she did.

If you are a tennis enthusiast, you might remember the 2009 Australian Open. An incredibly exciting five-set final between Roger Federer and Rafael Nadal. It was a Sunday so Peter was due to come to the vineyard for his usual lunch. He rang at about twelve o'clock to say he might be late because he couldn't tear himself away from the match; if I wasn't watching, turn it on immediately, it was fantastic tennis! I did, and it truly was beautiful tennis. Two world class players, ranked one and two, at the zenith of their abilities, battling point for point. Federer gliding about the court with perfect, effortless timing, opposite Nadal with his enormous strength, chasing the ball about the court with the speed of a cat and slamming it back at full reach. Each point was exhausting to watch. The games went on and on, tantalizingly close. Finally, Nadal made the break and won by a whisker. A tearful Roger Federer conceded defeat.

It was a cold, raw February day with snow in the air. Nevertheless, as a ritual, Peter liked to have a cold lager before his liver and bacon. The lager was on ice and the bacon crispy. The liver was waiting to be shown the foaming buttery pan at the last minute. Peter was never late for any event, a Major in the Cameron Highlanders to his fingertips.

Peter had an aneurysm, a permanent swelling of, in his case, the main artery from the heart. He could have had a huge operation and that part of the artery exchanged with a synthetic tube. But his platelet count was very low so any bleeding would be very difficult to stem. His friends told him at his age, ninety-three by now, and still with a relatively active life, an aneurysm was a merciful thing to have. When it burst, which it would do sooner rather than later there would be no pain and he'd die in thirty seconds.

He'd been with Carmen in her 'home' and my mother in hers. Although all the staff were kind and gentle, the whole idea of being 'looked-after' like that horrified him. Nevertheless to be told you'll suddenly die sometime soon, at whatever age you are, is a strange sensation to take on-board. Early on, soon after his diagnosis, we talked about it quite a lot, and he was issued with a panic button he wore around his neck, and he had a stairlift installed.

I've told you how interested he was in everything so to wallow around being introspective was not his style at all. Doing as much as we did together, his diagnosis receded to the back of our minds.

However, today he was late, we looked at each other and it sprang to the fore. We rang. No reply. He might be on his way. We waited five minutes. How could five minutes take so long? We quickly climbed into the car. As an afterthought, my wife put my chair in the back of the car. On arrival, all around the garden was still and quiet, his car in the garage. My wife gingerly pressed the front doorbell, nothing. Sensing the stillness of the garden, she carefully crept around the little cottage to the glass garden door. She cupped her hands to her face against the glare and peered in. There, on the floor, between his armchair and the television, was a little grey head.

Gently, head bowed, she walked back to the car. Holding my hands, she whispered, 'He's dead.' After a moment of stillness, she quickly hauled my chair out of the back of the car to my open driver's door. I dragged myself in as fast as possible. It had always been difficult to get me into the cottage, as the front doorstep was much higher than average. Then the lip at the top of the step was difficult for even a man to achieve, let alone my poor little wife.

Only with my mother, had I been in a room with a dead person, and now Peter. Two people so close, so full of life, so valuable, and now lifeless, completely still, nothing, gone, a shell, an empty shell. I feel sure I had an awareness of an empty space they left within my own body.

I couldn't get to the telephone so my wife rang 999 to report his death. The woman, immediately, very forcefully started barking instructions down the line. 'Get him flat on his back.' My wife said, 'I can't, I can't, he's dead.' 'How do you know he is dead? You're not in a position to know he is dead. Pull him flat on his back and pump the area in the middle of his chest until the police arrive.' 'I'll try, I'll try.' She couldn't, his fixed arm, he'd lost his elbow in a car crash while a cadet, was jammed around the end of the arm of his easy chair. The police did arrive incredibly quickly. They immediately summed up the situation and unassertively but firmly, took charge, two excellent policemen.

It was a freezing, snowing Sunday evening. Our local surgery was not on duty. The death had to be certified before removing the body from the site. The nearest ambulance for the task was Eastbourne, miles away. The two young policemen had to remain there to sign Peter over to the ambulance.

The snow started to lie heavily on the ground. The ambulance was making slow progress. We might not get safely down our drive and back to the Barn. If we got stuck on the way home, there'd be no assistance. We couldn't risk the possibility. We asked the two policemen if they could stay without us under these circumstances. 'Of course, of course, no problem at all, we have to stay anyway. The body can be transferred to any undertaker you wish after it's been to the morgue in Eastbourne.' Thank goodness we left then. By the morning, the snow was so thick we couldn't move anywhere for about a week.

My wife and the undertaker organised a beautiful funeral. A lot of people from all walks of Peter's life came to the crematorium. Carmen's godson gave the eulogy. My little sister's eldest daughter Kate read out letters Peter had written to his commanding officer during a posting in Belgrade. They epitomised the sharpness of his character, the attention to detail and his wit in social encounters. The army sent him to Cambridge University for six months to learn to write and understand Russian. Only six months. It was with that ability he was sent to the Russian sector in Belgrade. The entertaining of the Russian officers' wives, equally as important, was left up to Carmen. He and Carmen suited each other as a hand in a glove.

Peter would never have wanted a funeral exalting him in all the many diverse areas he found himself through the whole of his life. But that's what he deserved. So it was particularly clever of my wife, to orchestrate a funeral that was understated yet had all the elements that made him such an outstanding individual. We have cause to think of him every day.

Home Alone

Peter's solicitor attended the funeral, so I was able to give her all his files he'd put together for me, on one of the Sunday's he'd come for lunch. With his efficiency, she was able to complete probate in three months. She surprised even herself.

After all the organisation of the funeral and the house full of family (we have three spare bedrooms) we were shattered. We needed to be alone. Nevertheless, it was a strange sensation. Peter was the last of his generation for whom we were responsible. Not only the last of mine, my wife had no one left on her side either. All of us, at our age, are just one stage away from being a problem to the generation below us, our children or our nephews and nieces. Somebody is going to have to decide what to do with us. Each of us, one by one, will drop off our perches. I think most of us might be quite relieved not to have the responsibility of running a house or a business, but the expense of keeping us all alive for no effect or use to society, I can't help thinking is a terrible waste of resources. I realise the industry set up to keep us all alive is worth billions, but who do we benefit? What use are we? We serve no purpose. We have nothing to offer. I realise Peter benefited us hugely, but that's very unusual, and what use am I? I serve no purpose and haven't done so for years. Jokingly I say, at the age of eighty, or before if necessary, I'd like the vet to come to my house and put me down. In fact, I'm not really joking at all. I don't see why I shouldn't die at a time of my own choosing. My life is my own.

The next undertaking was Peter's little cottage. He'd said you must do with it whatever you think is best. We didn't want to sell it. It was too valuable to sell. But we had to clear it out and bring it up to date. Although he'd maintained the essentials, basically, it was exactly the same as when they first moved in, forty years before.

He told us what there was of any value, so to go through everything else would have taken forever, and inevitably been very depressing. We asked the auctioneer who came to value the contents for death duty, to recommend a house clearing firm he'd dealt with himself.

There are times in your life when you have a feeling you're making the wrong decision, but you can't quite figure why? This was one of those times. When we first met this man, I thought he was someone we could trust. My wife was hesitant. I should have listened to her and put a stop to him before he started, so simple. Interview someone else.

He and his team served their purpose in that they cleared out the house completely, over a weekend, with no exchange of money. We told him the deal did not include a set of very treasured china plates Peter had always told us about. He'd kept them hidden in a particular place which we couldn't reach. We told him where they were and he agreed he'd give them to us when he got there. You'll probably say I was naive, but I trusted him. My wife didn't, although she couldn't put her finger on it exactly, but she didn't think she liked him. Feminine intuition is a very complicated process for a mere man to follow, however hard you try. If she'd said, 'I definitely don't trust him,' I would, of course, have accepted her verdict. But she wasn't definite until the beginning of the second day.

At the end of the first day, he blustered into the room and more or less threw a plate on the table at which we were sitting, saying in an unnecessarily aggressive manner, 'There's your valuable china for you.'

My wife made up her mind overnight to confront him first thing on the Sunday morning. You can imagine the indignation it caused. He stormed out of the room in high dudgeon. It wasn't only him who'd effectively been accused of theft, it was his whole team two women and a man. The two women burst into tears and threatened to leave the site. No one had ever treated them in such an atrocious manner. I find it very difficult to believe he actually stole a set of china so blatantly and he would have had to have the cooperation of his whole team. It wouldn't have been worth their while. But why would Uncle Peter always have told us so precisely where the set was hidden, and why would the house clearer have given us just one plate? We also had the photographs Uncle Peter had taken off the whole set in case of theft. In this extraordinary confrontation, somebody had to give way. He couldn't, because he'd have to admit to theft. It was up to us to either follow it up or to give way. It made sense we should take the course of the latter, to get the job done.

Apart from that unfortunate start to owning it, the cottage has brought nothing but happiness to all those who have tenanted it. So much so, they all have assumed they had the right to buy it.

One day it will be sold with our whole estate, but meanwhile it serves us very well as it is. It's a very strange awareness that in ten years I'll be eighty-two and my wife will be eighty. All old people look like old people, and we will be just the same. Strangely though, my little wife, looks exactly the same as she did when her friend Camilla brought her to the Kedong valley in nineteen sixty-five. She still has an hourglass figure and her skin is flawless and she hasn't a grey hair on her head. How is it everyone else looks their age when my wife looks exactly the same as she ever did? It must be because of the quiet, uneventful, trouble free life we've led!

On one occasion when my mother-in-law was still alive we, and my wife's brother and children, were staying with her for the weekend. Natasha, my brother-in-law's daughter, who must have about ten years old said, completely un-maliciously, quietly, as her grandmother slowly crept into the room, 'Here comes Crumple.' She'd never called her that before and I'm not aware she ever did so again. But that little anecdote only serves to emphasise how all elderly people are regarded by the younger generation. I don't think my mother-in-law was any older than I am now

On our 'round the world' trip in our beautiful little ship the Saga Ruby, we stopped at the small South Korean island of Jeju. We're both fascinated by the intricacy of bonsai trees. The work entailed in the tending of the aged trees, however old they may be, will have had to be tended by someone practically every day of their lives. They can't be left to look after themselves in the way our ordinary everyday trees are. You could have a bonsai oak or beech or any of our English trees, but they can't be left to look after themselves all the year round. In winter, during their dormancy, they won't need everyday care, but if you have more than a few, there'll be a cycle of work that'll be called for on a regular basis. Every two or three years they need to be taken out of their pots to have their roots pruned. In the summer, they must be watered twice every day.

One of the trips organised by the Ship was a visit to a bonsai garden. It was very cold weather so we were the only people on this expedition. The solitude and quietness of these ancient trees gave an immense gravity to the whole garden. It instantly swept us back more than fifty years to that old, old orchard in which we pitched our tent in northern Greece. This was on our trip back to England, before we were married, being chaperoned by Honey through the Middle East. All the trees were set about glittering, clear, wandering waterways, teeming with huge, lazily swimming, golden koi carp. We could only smile with deep warmth as we slowly moved about the breathtaking beauty of these ancient trees.

The couple who looked after our house while we were away for all that time, Chris and Gilly, are aficionados for finding the best places to eat fish and chips. This time they recommended a pub near Bodiam Castle. They were right. The fish and chips were delicious. It was a lovely day, so after lunch we thought we'd do what we've come to love doing at this late onset of our lives, slowly driving around English country lanes trying to get lost. Fairly soon we passed a little sign, simply saying, 'Bodiam bonsai'. We stopped. That 'stop' has turned out to be the most expensive 'stop' we've made since spotting the advert for sailing around the world!

Our collection has outgrown the courtyard garden. Every pillar has its own tree. All the other trees, I'm not quite sure how many, have created their own garden, leading on from the rose garden, which my wife planted in memory of my mother.

These trees are sitting on their own half ton, uncut, rough, natural slate, triangular rocks, from a slate quarry in Cornwall. The appearance and age of the rocks enhance the age and beauty of the trees. The rocks are the waste product at the top of a new quarry, rusty brown slate, before getting to the clear grey slate we all know. The rocks are set out at random, about six to eight feet apart, in a high-fenced area about one hundred foot square. The fence has to be both rabbit proof and deer proof. The trees are irresistible to vegetarian nibblers. The rabbits are particularly destructive, because they climb up inside the tree, using it as a perch, and eat it from inside out.

Between all the rocks, will be planted wildflowers from all around the Wealden area. All the trees have their own drip feed watering system, controlled by clocks at the main source of the water. I have an electric wheelchair so I can easily visit each tree to work on it. As some of the trees are quite tall, which differs from tree to tree, the seat of the chair rises so I can reach the top of the taller trees for pruning. It takes quite a few years to 'know' a tree well, so by the time I do, I'll be very close to the end of my borrowed time. That time so easily could have come to its conclusion, just outside the ramshackle little dry, dusty township of Rumaruti, in the north of Kenya, at five o'clock in the afternoon, on the twenty ninth of June, nineteen seventy six.

***

This must be the final chapter, as now there's a glimmer, still quite far away, at the end of a very long tunnel. It's a faint speck, a little dot in the distance, signifying the end. Not just the end of my story, I also see the end of me. Through years of despair and torment, I longed for the end, and now I can see it. I think we've achieved quite a lot, but without my little wife pushing, lifting, straining, nurturing, I wouldn't have achieved anything.

Now that I can see the end, I find I'm quite comforted by it, even liberated. Living so close to the endings of my mother, Carmen and Peter, I know the actual 'death' itself isn't something of which I need to be fearful, but the run up to that moment is usually pretty awful. Peter's was very quick; he was never bed-bound by weakness or illness. He thought about stopping smoking occasionally, but as he'd never suffered anything, not even so much as a cough, he let the thought go. He never smoked while in our house, or in our car, even though he'd given it to us. We have a photograph of him and Carmen's godson, Tats, standing outside, in the dark, snow-covered courtyard, puffing away before being allowed back in! I think I might as well continue drinking slightly more than the recommended allowance of red wine per day, especially as I'm now the full-time chef. And as for taking a break once a week, forget it!

I'm told I should finish on an upbeat note, but I've tried to tell you, perhaps too graphically at times, how it actually is, leading the life of a paraplegic. Inevitably that must be 'down' rather than 'up'. But you can take it either way.

I lived a magical childhood that contrasted somewhat with my undeniably 'wanting' education. However, it did lead me by a circuitous, contorted route to an acting career at the Donovan Maule theatre in Nairobi and meeting my beautiful little wife in the Kedong valley. This was a fortuitous and thrilling meeting for me, but a fateful, even disastrous meeting for her, in view of what has happened to me since.

I've told you how lucky we've been meeting so many incredibly kind and generous people everywhere we've been. It's hard to believe the enormity of help, encouragement and love we've received from friends and family. I can only thank them all from the bottom of my heart.

We're now settled and satisfied with our life, as I was in my magical childhood home in the Kedong Valley. I can still take myself back there in a moment, standing on the moss covered rocks among all the ferns and the huge shiny, broadleaf water lilies in the shade of enormous wild fig trees, warm water rising up out of the ground and tumbling through the rocks to the long natural pool full of freshwater fish. But I have no yearning to do so any more. We've created a beauty and peace from a derelict old wooden barn, with bluebell woods, gardens and streams, just as my father and my mother did in 1945 at the source of the Kedong River.

I can't end my story without reiterating my love and gratitude to my wonderful little wife, without whom my life would be impossible. Her guidance and love have given me an inner strength to find my way through the darkest of times. She is in my heart and soul.

Thank you for bearing with me through the telling of this rather tortuous tale, and goodbye for now.

／

Acknowledgements

Hugely, unreservedly I thank Trevor, who quite suddenly popped up out of nowhere to become a close and trusted friend I seem to have known forever. Without him, this book would remain a pile of jumbled-up stories somewhere in my docs file! To begin with he persuaded my uncooperative computer to behave in a reasonable manner towards its distraught owner. Once a week Trevor visited us morning or afternoon and we'd chat about anything and everything. Then, more recently, the three of us would sit around the kitchen table making corrections to my previous week's work but no alterations to sentiment or story was allowed.

This book isn't the only project we've undertaken. The first project was to build a 1 to 7 scale model of a Tiger Moth biplane. Every detail was exact. After three months work, I held the completed craft tightly aloft for Trevor to start the engine. It powered into life the first time. Everything else worked perfectly with the remote control. The rudder, the wing flaps, the power of the engine, everything. We were ready for our maiden flight. But that's as far as we dared go. All that work for a crash landing in minutes. No, no, no. It now hangs from a beam high up in our barn sitting room looking as though it were in midflight. Without Trevor, it wouldn't be there. As with this book, without Trevor it would not be here.

Lightning Source UK Ltd.
Milton Keynes UK
UKOW05f0704280617
304210UK00001B/4/P